Pa

Colin Root

Paul Thomas Anderson

from Hard Eight to Punch-Drunk Love

Lambert Academic Publishing

Impressum/Imprint (nur für Deutschland/ only for Germany)

Bibliografische Information der Deutschen Nationalbibliothek: Die Deutsche Nationalbibliothek verzeichnet diese Publikation in der Deutschen Nationalbibliografie; detaillierte bibliografische Daten sind im Internet über http://dnb.d-nb.de abrufbar.

Alle in diesem Buch genannten Marken und Produktnamen unterliegen warenzeichen-, marken- oder patentrechtlichem Schutz bzw. sind Warenzeichen oder eingetragene Warenzeichen der jeweiligen Inhaber. Die Wiedergabe von Marken, Produktnamen, Gebrauchsnamen, Handelsnamen, Warenbezeichnungen u.s.w. in diesem Werk berechtigt auch ohne besondere Kennzeichnung nicht zu der Annahme, dass solche Namen im Sinne der Warenzeichen- und Markenschutzgesetzgebung als frei zu betrachten wären und daher von jedermann benutzt werden dürften.

Verlag: Lambert Academic Publishing AG & Co. KG
Theodor-Heuss-Ring 26, 50668 Köln, Deutschland
Telefon +49 681 3720-310, Telefax +49 681 3720-3109, Email: info@lap-publishing.com

Herstellung in Deutschland:
Schaltungsdienst Lange o.H.G., Berlin
Books on Demand GmbH, Norderstedt
Reha GmbH, Saarbrücken
Amazon Distribution GmbH, Leipzig
ISBN: 978-3-8383-2255-1

Imprint (only for USA, GB)

Bibliographic information published by the Deutsche Nationalbibliothek: The Deutsche Nationalbibliothek lists this publication in the Deutsche Nationalbibliografie; detailed bibliographic data are available in the Internet at http://dnb.d-nb.de.

Any brand names and product names mentioned in this book are subject to trademark, brand or patent protection and are trademarks or registered trademarks of their respective holders. The use of brand names, product names, common names, trade names, product descriptions etc. even without a particular marking in this works is in no way to be construed to mean that such names may be regarded as unrestricted in respect of trademark and brand protection legislation and could thus be used by anyone.

Publisher:
Lambert Academic Publishing AG & Co. KG
Theodor-Heuss-Ring 26, 50668 Köln, Germany
Phone +49 681 3720-310, Fax +49 681 3720-3109, Email: info@lap-publishing.com

Printed in the U.S.A.
Printed in the U.K. by (see last page)
ISBN: 978-3-8383-2255-1

TABLE OF CONTENTS

INTRODUCTION: THE CHOICE OF THE AMERICAN FILM ARTIST

Occasionally, the experience of a film can transcend the conventions of cinematic form and open doors to a new world of artistic expression. In fact, the artist's primary concern is offering a new perspective on the nature of man and the world in which he lives. When we are given a new view of the world by an artist, our initial reactions are often a combination of shock, confusion, and mistrust. Sometimes, this confusion is never overcome, and great art is left unrecognized. Other times, an artist's contribution to his medium is acknowledged as a singular, original vision of the world, and changes the lives of those who have contact with it. The history of American film has produced many such works of art. However, given the nature of the American film industry's proclivity toward a cinema of entertainment, the great works of film art are usually found in artistic circles outside of the Hollywood studio system.

This relatively independent cinema in the United States takes on three dominant forms. First, there are film artists who steadfastly reject narrative filmmaking, and approach an avant-garde cinema, unconcerned with audiences, box office, or reviews and criticism. They are artists who work simply for the enjoyment of creative expression. Secondly, there are independent narrative filmmakers, who look to festivals and small theater circuits to showcase their work. These filmmakers are also distanced from the dominant Hollywood system by small budgets or the use of non-professional cast and crew. Lastly, there are directors who express their independent vision by *using* the Hollywood system itself. These filmmakers occupy a paradoxical relationship with mainstream American cinema. They work within Hollywood's confines (i.e. budgetary concerns, use of stars, modest box office expectations), but offer an alternative vision to the mainstream narrative, which is a cinema based on the achievement of goals and resolution of conflict. The second and third categories are not to be interchanged for any understanding of the requirements and limitations of independent filmmaking. The second group chooses to work outside the studio system for greater freedom of personal expression, both thematically and stylistically. While some of film's best performances fall within this category, their limited appeal and rawness of style prevents them to impact mainstream culture in any significant way. However, the third group seeks to combine the freedom of true independent cinema with the benefits of studio money and personnel. This is the category into which Paul Thomas Anderson and other directors of the New American Cinema fall.

But new forms of expression mean a departure from certain aspects of dominant film culture. Above all, the artist must offer an intensely personal, unique vision of the world. The Russian filmmaker Andrei Tarkovsky writes in *Sculpting in Time* that works of art should prepare us for death. At their best, works of art are meant to present an audience with a deeper understanding of humanity. It is this human element that allows great masterpieces to affect us personally and profoundly. When one is confronted with a work of art, it should serve man's desire to know himself. Thus, when we can recognize the vision of the world given to us by an artist, the work ceases to function only as an independent entity, and assumes the role of a gauge by which we check our sense of the world. The work of Paul Thomas Anderson is interested in showing us a world in which people are at the center of the way to higher consciousness. As most Hollywood cinema is based on action and goal attainment, the character-driven narrative seeks to deal with the experiences that would seem commonplace or unexciting in a mainstream film. Anderson is a director whose primary concern is to show the audience itself. Although deeply flawed, his characters are not constructed to evoke pity, be the objects of our condescension, or perform superhuman heroics. Rather, Anderson's characters, like all of us, are products of our own successes and mistakes. Despite their eccentricities, Anderson's characters share commonalities with us not through action or plot, but by theme—pain, redemption, love, or sin. Instead of being locked into a single mode of behavior, the characters in Anderson's films fluctuate rapidly in tone and mood. By doing so, they avoid compartmentalization as a 'type'—the brain, the drug addict, the straight man, etc. Instead, by constantly shifting from one persona to another, they maintain their emotional autonomy and unpredictability. In a Paul Thomas Anderson film, we are kept from judging the characters or from standing above them emotionally. In the hands of such an artist, we are presented with a vision of the world that compels us to turn our view inward, to examine and appreciate the complexities and ambiguities of life.

Paul Thomas Anderson was born on January 1, 1970, the first day of the new decade. He grew up in Studio City, California in the San Fernando Valley outside Los Angeles, and had always been interested in the entertainment industry. His father, Ernie Anderson, had been a local celebrity in Cleveland for a radio show, in which he played a character named 'Ghoulardi'.[1] His father would play an important role in exposing Paul to actors and other people involved in the entertainment industry. Growing up in Southern California, Paul worked as a production assistant on several films during his teen years. He often experimented with making his own films with a video camera, and made a mockumentary called 'The Dirk Diggler Story' in 1988, which would later become the basis for *Boogie Nights*. Although he had always been somewhat indifferent to the notion of film school, Paul entered New York University's Tisch School for the Arts in 1990 to learn film production, but quit after only two days. Paul spent the next few years working odd jobs on sets and making contacts with actors who would later work with Paul on his first productions, most significantly Robert Ridgely and Philip Baker Hall. With the money scraped together from reimbursed tuition and production assistant jobs, Paul made a short film entitled *Cigarettes and Coffee* in 1993. The film would end up at the Sundance Film Festival later that year, where it played in the short film category. The 30-minute film centers on three conversations in a diner. The first situation deals with a young man expressing the desire to kill his wife to an older man (Philip Baker Hall). At a nearby table, there is an agitated, malicious husband, and a remorseful, submissive wife arguing about her gambling addiction. The third conversation involves a man on a pay phone talking about an unexplained plan. The film is unpolished dramatically, and the acting is overstated at certain points. Nevertheless, the interest of the film lies in its directorial style—the dollying camera and the use of lines and symmetry in a shot—which are techniques that Anderson will repeat in each of his subsequent films. (Most significantly, *Cigarettes and Coffee* anticipates the dramatic tone of *Hard Eight*. In fact, the setting of Anderson's short film greatly resembles the opening sequence between John and Sydney at Jack's Coffee Shop in *Hard Eight*.)

After *Cigarettes and Coffee* was shown at Sundance, Anderson received the invitation that was to mark the beginning of his career in independent film. Beginning at the age of twenty-three, Anderson would spend the next two years of his life determined to break into feature filmmaking.

The gods visit the sins of the fathers upon the children.

—Euripides

That is the thankless position of the father in the family—
the provider for all, and the enemy of all.

—August Strindberg, 1886
"The Son of a Servant"

CHAPTER 1

HARD EIGHT (1996): THE SINS OF THE FATHER

While *Cigarettes and Coffee* was playing at Sundance, Anderson expanded the short's script into a 90-minute screenplay entitled *Sydney*. The Festival's program director Michelle Satter read the script and invited Anderson to work at the Sundance Institute's Filmmaker Workshop Lab under the tutelage of such Hollywood directors as John Schlesinger and Michael Caton-Jones. *Hard Eight*[2] was to be Anderson's first feature-length project. For a film school dropout, the opportunity to work on his own feature project with a decent budget seemed too good to be true, which, to a certain degree, was the case. Looking back on the Sundance experience, Anderson recalls, "If you're a first-time filmmaker, and you've got someone to give you the money, you're going to take it. Don't. It's better not to make your movie. If it's smells fishy, don't fucking get involved."[3] It was the hard concessions he forfeited on *Hard Eight* that made Anderson push harder for control over his future productions.

In relation to what was to follow in Anderson's *oeuvre*, the script for *Hard Eight* was a small and intimate story, in which even many of the action sequences seem restrained. But despite his interest in making something different from standard Hollywood fare, Anderson had not yet decided what type of filmmaker he wanted to become. Reflecting on the period of making *Hard Eight*, Anderson says, "I knew that my sensibility wasn't incredibly art house, and I knew that my sensibility wasn't incredibly *Batman*."[4] It would be the struggle between these two forces that would characterize all of Anderson's work to come. Nevertheless, it is difficult to place Anderson (after *Cigarettes and Coffee*) into the 'American Independent Film'

6

category. Anderson is the first to admit that he approaches each film with a commercial sensibility. Like many new American directors of the 1990s, Anderson unequivocally wants his films to reach mainstream audiences. His biggest fear was for *Hard Eight* to play small art house theatres and disappear into oblivion. It is in this respect that the Sundance experience was most influential on Anderson. The Screenwriters Lab taught him how to avoid making a script too small for a commercial audience, while still achieving the movie he wanted. Although the Institute had a clear agenda of turning talented independent filmmakers into bankable directors, the method of production at the Lab did not work like a studio. Instead, the Lab existed to polish the skills of promising young directors, allowing room for error, since the financial stakes were relatively low by Hollywood terms. Anderson recalls a conversation with the Lab's Artistic Director Jeremy Kagan in which he was told, "You're here to fuck up, and then to fuck up better the next day."[5] As Anderson reworked the script for *Hard Eight* in 1994, it was clear that his ideas required a feature-length film to be effective.

As with *Cigarettes and Coffee*, Anderson wanted Philip Baker Hall for the lead role of Sydney in *Hard Eight*. As Anderson recalls, *Hard Eight* was not an outgrowth of *Cigarettes and Coffee*, but "grew out of the same actor [Hall]."[6] He once called Hall "*the* great American actor"[7] and credits him as the reason he wrote *Hard Eight* in the first place. Likewise, the part of John was written specifically with a young actor in mind, John C. Reilly, who had had only a few small roles before Anderson asked him to play the lead in *Hard Eight*.[8] Anderson's method is to simultaneously be an awestruck fan and a personal ally of his actors. Reilly described Anderson as the most emotionally involved director with whom he has worked. He says that Anderson crouches nervously by the camera, and once "cut" is called, runs over to the actors excitedly with praise or suggestions on how it could work differently. In late 1994, Hall and Reilly accompanied Anderson to the Sundance Lab, where the script was workshopped and run through dress rehearsals in preparation for shooting. Anderson supplemented the cast of Hall and Reilly with Gwyneth Paltrow and Samuel L. Jackson, a bankable actor coming off Quentin Tarantino's *Pulp Fiction* (1994). Anderson, Hall, and Reilly had waited for the script to *Hard Eight* to get the green light since 1993. In the meantime, Anderson had been offered more money to allow someone else to direct the film and to replace Hall and Reilly with bigger stars.[9] But for a movie that was character-driven and dependent on acting, Anderson recognized that he needed expressive faces and actors who understood the script, rather than big names in the leads. Moreover, Reilly and Hall had had the script in hand for three years — adequate time to understand the characters of John and Sydney. Reilly and Hall improvised much of their performances at Sundance, which became integral to Anderson's final script. Anderson says, "It started as a blueprint for the actors to mess around with. By the time they were done with it, a lot of mysteries were cleared up."[10]

Principal photography began in January 1995 in Reno, Nevada and lasted twenty-eight days. After shooting wrapped in February, Anderson recalls a disastrous process of editing, in which executives at Rysher Entertainment attempted to regain control of the picture's editing.[11] This struggle would eventually cost Anderson final cut on the film, in addition to changing its title from *Sydney* to *Hard Eight*. Anderson's nightmare had, to some extent, come true. Anderson adds:

> What they were trying to teach me at the Lab, which I was probably too silly to listen to, is that only fifty percent of my job was to write and direct good movies. The other fifty percent was dealing with people who pay for movies and dealing with the distribution process.[12]

By 1996, the Sundance Festival had become a deal-making juggernaut for Hollywood producers, searching for the next promising director coming out of the independent ranks. By choosing to work under the umbrella of Hollywood's financing, Anderson's personal vision was greatly compromised by the pressure put on him by the moneychangers. To Anderson's disappointment, the film finally opened on January 20, 1996 at the Sundance Film Festival and later in relatively few art cinemas (29 screens in all) around the country with little fanfare. After a brief run, the film grossed just under $150,000.

Anderson readily admits that he often has trouble thinking of how to begin a new film.[13] In *Hard Eight*, he wanted to forgo the prologue and begin the development of his characters. Because he already knew Sydney's character, the supporting roles essentially grew out of a response to Sydney. Anderson's theory about beginning a script is: "If you don't know what you're writing, just put two people in a coffee shop, and have them start talking, and it will eventually figure itself out."[14] This is essentially how Anderson begins *Hard Eight*. The first image is outside of Jack's Coffee Shop in Reno, a scene that begins with a shadowy figure approaching a young man seated outside the restaurant from across the parking lot.

8

Anderson establishes the technique of withholding visual information from the viewer, which will reappear frequently throughout *Hard Eight*. The camera, placed at knee level, follows the figure all the way across the lot to the young man, until they each fill half of the frame. As we hear the stranger's voice ask the young man to join him for cigarettes and coffee, the lack of introduction to the unseen man makes the audience and the young man skeptical of his motives. However, the film does not stay in this tone for longer than their initial encounter. With the first cut of the film, Anderson reverses the suspense he has created with the previous scene outside between Sydney and John, cutting directly to a close-up of both men already seated in the restaurant. The ensuing conversation shows Anderson's desire to let us see inwardly into his characters. In fact, the intimacy of the characters' initial conversation reveals much about Anderson as a director – that if he can hold an audience's attention with two characters sitting and talking about mundane things, then the scene has accomplished its goals. This idea can be seen throughout Anderson's films, as he shows us his affinity for the pleasure of listening to interesting conversations between dynamic characters.

Anderson is interested in exploring people who have been marginalized in American culture. Nevertheless, he prefers the type of film that expresses genuine emotions and a generally optimistic vision of humanity. His characters are rarely presented with ironic or caricatured inflections in *Hard Eight*, but rather, deal with people who confront serious problems in the hope of repairing their damaged lives. The characters in *Hard Eight* are given an autonomous identity and a set of guiding principles that operate independently of other characters. In this way, acting in Anderson's films resembles true-to-life interaction, in which we are constantly responding to others based on moment-by-moment feelings. The interest of a Paul Thomas Anderson film comes in the tones and internalizations of emotion that occur in conversation. Anderson's characters tell their stories through awkward silences, darting eyes or impulsive confessions.

The narrative centers on four main characters, interconnected through chance encounters in Reno. Sydney is a lifelong gambler, who maintains a classy exterior despite his true financial situation. Anderson says, "Sydney's sort of a grinder around town. He lives off the benefits and comps of casinos…he's set for the next six months."[15] He feels most comfortable in the environs of the casino, and confidently strolls the casino floors, playing just enough to get by. John is a naïve drifter who needs money to bury his mother. He is a young man, eager to learn the ways of beating the system from Sydney, to whom he looks as a mentor. Clementine is a waitress and a prostitute at the casino. She is headstrong, but also imprudent and seeks comfort by attaching herself to the men in the film. Jimmy is a hustler in town who follows the money around. He is a crude man looking for respect from those he encounters. With the interactions between these characters, Anderson does not want to establish a unidirectional mode of behavior for each character, but rather to show each person fluctuating between the extremes of human emotions.

During this conversation in the film's opening sequence, the tone of their exchange shifts moment by moment, as the viewer gathers scraps of information about both men. In the following sequence, each character fluctuates between moments of maintaining a tough façade and revealing vulnerability:

> SYDNEY: (probing) You lost some money?
> JOHN: (indignant) No.
> SYDNEY: (sarcastically) You won some money?
> JOHN: (coldly) I broke even.
> SYDNEY: What were you playing?
> JOHN: Blackjack.
> SYDNEY: (businesslike) You know how to count cards?
> JOHN: (uninterested) What?
> SYDNEY: (haughty) You said you were playing blackjack. Do you know how to count cards?
> JOHN: (serious) No.
> SYDNEY: (condescending) In my experience, if you don't know how to count cards, you ought to stay away from blackjack.
> JOHN: (hurt and angry) Well, thanks for the tip, Mr. Helpful.
> SYDNEY: (reprimanding) Hey John.
> JOHN: (indifferent) What?
> SYDNEY: (wounded pride) Hey John. I'm sitting here. I've bought you a cup of coffee, given you a cigarette. (scolding) Hey John, look at me. If you want to be a wiseass, go outside and take a seat. (tenderly) But if you want to talk to me, if you want to *talk* to me, well then...(instructively) never ignore a man's courtesy.

What makes *Hard Eight*'s characters complex is this variability of personality, in which tones reverse and switch rapidly within a single scene. Anderson is concerned with the way people cover hurt feelings with performance and how true emotional expression necessitates a Herculean effort. In the above exchange, the audience understands John's embarrassment at asking Sydney, a total stranger, for help. As the film cuts between the two men talking, the camera moves increasingly closer to the eyes of both John and Sydney. Partly due to the unique characteristics of the faces of Hall and Reilly, the inflections of their faces and body language, not their words, become the emotional indicators of the scene. Sydney stares intently into John's eyes, almost always maintaining eye contact. Conversely, John's eyes continually dart back and forth in shame or nervousness at each of Sydney's questions. It would initially seem that Anderson intends to establish an aggressive/submissive relationship between the two men. This theory is strengthened by Sydney's paternal chiding: "You want to be a wiseass, go outside and take a seat, but if you want to talk to me, if you want to *talk* to me...never ignore a man's courtesy." But as their dialogue continues, John's honesty about needing money to bury his mother endears him to Sydney and John begins to assert his problems with more eloquence and urgency. As John's tones alternate between pride, hurtfulness, and resignation with each response, we understand that he desires Sydney's help despite his superficial indifference. Although John's responses total less than fifteen words in this entire exchange, the film has already given us several emotional clues as to the state of his psychology. Likewise, Sydney's tones move from condescension to tenderness and back again within a single sentence. Anderson has refused to give us a road map of either man's emotional path, but rather a meandering, moment-by-moment interplay of action and reaction. The result is a sense of urgency, a tension that exists under their words, as if everything rests on the outcome of their discussion. This is a device that Anderson uses in each of his films to create a level of suspense that drives the narrative forward. As the two men talk, smoke drifts upward from the cigarettes and coffee on the table, rising and almost enveloping both men, visually adding a sense of importance to their words. Although the scene contains no action, but only dialogue, Anderson wants to inject the film with visual excitement that will hold our attention while we listen.

Although their conversation maintains a certain level of gravity, Anderson interjects a comedic exchange toward the end of their talk. When Sydney invites John to come back to Vegas with him, John replies that he knows three types of karate, implying that he still does not trust Sydney's unmotivated benevolence. He adds that his conditions are, "A) You give me a ride, 2) You give me 50 bucks and C) I sit in the back." Although the audience laughs at John's apparent absurdity, John is completely resolute and forceful in his demands. It is important, though, that the film does not judge this moment negatively as sarcasm or condescension on the director's part. Anderson says, "It's great when actors can play characters who aren't so smart and they don't make a gag of it, don't condescend. Stupidity can be funny and real. It doesn't have to be jokey and fake."[16] As the two men set off together, the viewer is given the sense that John and Sydney are now inextricably bound.

11

We feel as if the pairing of Sydney with John is reconciliatory. Thus, Anderson has begun the film with sensations, playing on our use of intuition through unexplained relationships and characters that superficially have no bond. There is the sense that both are searching for something, and are willing to take a chance on one another in order to fulfill some need.

As the film progresses, the relationship between Sydney and John occasionally assumes a father/son coupling. In the first part of the film, John is completely dependent on Sydney for even basic needs—food, shelter, and money—as a child would be with a parent. John warms up quickly to Sydney on the road to Las Vegas, as Sydney drives and John rides in the backseat. Although the scene is initially humorous—John having followed through on his previous condition in Jack's Coffee Shop to sit in the back—the two men sit in near silence, exchanging only a few words. But what happens next is one of the most interesting stylistic moments in Anderson's young filmmaking career. After realizing that he can trust Sydney, John asks if Sydney can pull the car over. With a jump cut and the sound of a passing car horn, John appears in the front seat with a jump cut. Anderson later recalled that the decision to use the cut came from necessity, as the footage of John changing places in the car was ruined.[17] Necessity, it seems for Anderson, was the mother of invention. Nevertheless, the effect of the jump cut is to visually erase the emotional boundary that had existed between them until this point in the film.

The parent/child implication sheds light on one of Anderson's central thematic concerns in many of Anderson's films—the struggle to move forward while dealing with issues from the past. Anderson's films seem to look nostalgically to the past, giving a sense that something has been lost which can never be regained. Historically, this sort of subject matter has found a place in the theatre in the melancholic plays of Arthur Miller or Tennessee Williams. But the interest of Sydney's character does not lie in his unidirectional pursuit of recovering his past, but rather his inconsistencies in getting there. The point is to not let us get ahead of his present emotions, but to deal with them moment-by-moment in the film. In the first ten minutes of *Hard Eight*, nothing has been clarified about Sydney's or John's character, but more importantly, the viewer has no choice but to follow each exchange or set of events as they come.

Stylistically, Anderson made another formal discovery during the filming of this scene. During the ride to Las Vegas, as John describes his pants catching fire, Anderson had a conversation that would change his understanding of how to tell a story:

I sat down with Richard La Gravenese and he said, 'Why am I reading about this? Why am I not seeing it?' And I thought, 'Well, that's kind of incredible. Why don't I show it?' That's just a very basic thing, one really strong thing I took [from the Sundance Lab].[18]

This theory also applies to the subsequent scene between Sydney and John in a Las Vegas casino, as Sydney teaches John how to stretch his fifty-dollar loan into a meal and a free hotel room for the evening. During the filming of *Hard Eight*, Anderson recognized the effectiveness of *showing*, rather than talking. Regarding his direction, Anderson assesses his style in the following way:

I think I direct in a way that's technical and show-off-y, and that's not something that's generally said about writers who direct. With those sort of writers who direct, like David Mamet or Woody Allen, you don't usually think of them applying a lot of cinema—in the Scorsese or Oliver Stone kind of way—to their movies.[19]

This self-professed desire for technical showiness permeates each of Anderson's films. Anderson's framing, although realistic, presents us with a visual field that limits the characters. Almost every shot in *Hard Eight* places people within the context of their surroundings. Their bodies are framed by the spaces they inhabit. Anderson wants the viewer to get a sense of claustrophobia, of being boxed in by one's choices. It is a kind of visual drama at work, by which we are meant to feel the pressure of the confinement as the characters do.

This point is illustrated by the way Anderson photographs the casino (Reno's Peppermill Casino) in the opening sequence. The gambling sequences in *Hard Eight* illustrate the way that a casino looked to the young Anderson, who spent many evenings playing craps and bumming around Reno and Las Vegas in the early 1990s. In *Hard Eight*, Anderson always remains conscious of giving a realistic believability to his locations: "Most movies show a casino the way it is on Saturday night. I'm also trying to show it Tuesday at 6 p.m. The band isn't playing yet. It's kind of loose."[20]

Even in moments of relatively unconfined spaces, Anderson still maintains this sensation of captivity, something the film suggests needs to be done away with. The change in closeness of the two men in the car on the open road suggests that an emotional door has been opened for both John and Sydney. Although they exchange mostly banal chitchat about using matches, a shift occurs in John's demeanor. John begins to open himself to

Sydney by modifying his speech. He no longer exhibits the indignant, detached tone that he used in the coffee shop scene. John has let his guard down a bit and is no longer threatening as before ("I will fuck you up if you fuck with me"), but rather, reveals a more childlike, innocent quality during the matchbook story.[21] As John is explaining that he never uses matches because of an incident involving "spontaneous friction" while standing in a movie line, Anderson introduces a major theme in *Hard Eight*, as well as his entire *oeuvre*. As John finally recoils from his tough guy attitude regarding suing the match company, he says, "This happens, that happens, shit just happens, you just deal with it." In an Anderson film, characters "deal with it" in many ways. The notion of "spontaneous friction" applies directly to the relationship between John and Sydney, in which two souls are seeking contact with one another to produce new understandings. The point is that their encounter was not random or unimportant, but rather, that coincidental meetings can be significant life-changing experiences if one is open to a higher state of consciousness where emotional honesty and trust are not concealed.

Sydney's fatherliness is not limited only to his relationship with John. When Clementine, a waitress at the bar, engages Sydney in conversation at his table, Sydney again shows fatherly concern by inquiring about flirting for tips and acts protective of her, as if she were his daughter. The suggestion of a surrogate father/child relationship is strengthened by Clementine's nickname for Sydney—Captain. As with John, Sydney initially appears comfortable in his role as a warm and guiding fatherly presence to Clementine. At times, he lovingly coaches her through moments of indecision, offering advice, money, and solace. When Sydney sees Clementine coming out of a hotel room after an obvious prostitution call, the two go for coffee, where they discuss more intimate details about their private lives. Sydney tells Clementine that he has a son and daughter about the same ages as John and Clementine and reveals that he has not spoken to them in a long time. (An identical conversation will reoccur in *Magnolia* between Earl and Phil about Earl's lost son Frank.) Thus, we begin to understand Sydney's actions toward both John and Clementine to be motivated by a sense of loss and an attempt to recapture familial closeness, a concept that will repeat in Anderson's next two films.

However, the film does not allow Sydney to remain in his position of caregiver. When he teaches John the trick to getting a free hotel room at the casino, Sydney plays it as if he is untouchable, a man who knows all the angles. But to give Sydney complexity in *Hard Eight*,

14

Anderson's strategy is to create a doubleness in his character, a strategy he will use often in his films. The truth is that Sydney is not as dignified as he presents himself to be. But it is important to note that this doubleness is not presented as deceitful or even self-conscious. Sydney is not 'living a lie,' so to speak, but rather, instinctively maintains a degree of dignity in a world he knows, the casino floor. Anderson's point is that we are often unaware of the different masks we use in life and often retreat to a place of emotional safety when our masks are called into question. A fundamental interest of Anderson's films is expressed in the gap that exists between our true selves and what we show to the outside world.

Consequently, with the introduction of Jimmy, Sydney's paternal, seemingly impenetrable façade begins to show signs of vulnerability underneath. Near the end of the film, as Jimmy holds Sydney for ransom, Anderson reveals Sydney's doubleness: "You walk around like you're Mr. Cool, Mr. Wisdom, but you're not. You're just some old hood." Jimmy is the only character who sees through Sydney's cool exterior, and therefore, threatens to unmask Sydney's outward image of himself. Sydney is immediately put off by Jimmy's crudity and we instantly identify Jimmy as boorish and unsophisticated, a foil for Sydney's poised façade. However, Anderson is again cautious not to allow us to oversimplify his characters. During the initial conversation between Sydney and Jimmy, a significant tonal shift occurs. Jimmy seizes power from Sydney by insinuating that Sydney gave up being a high-profile gambler to play Keno. This insult begins to expose Sydney's weakness, the shame of being past his prime and not always the polished sophisticate he imagines he is. Sydney retaliates by suggesting that Jimmy is merely a parking lot attendant, rather than casino security. The viewer understands this power struggle as male posturing in their exchanging of tones, in which both men fight to maintain their dignity. When Jimmy and John leave the table, Sydney walks alone to a craps table and begins gambling. As the film gives the viewer a moment alone with Sydney, we understand that Jimmy's words have stung Sydney, and he retreats to his safe world on the casino floor. This is the first indication (but not the last) that Sydney maintains these multiple masks. This is a kind of suspense mechanism on Anderson's part, as he warns us to look for further chinks in Sydney's emotional armor.

The insecurity that Jimmy has exposed in Sydney resurfaces just a few scenes later as Sydney gambles alone in the casino. As he plays craps, he is rattled into placing a $2,000 bet on the 'hard eight' by a young loudmouth (Philip Seymour Hoffman). This is the exact bet that Jimmy said that Sydney *used* to make when he had seen him years before. With this contrivance, the film wants to be absolutely clear that we understand Sydney's frustration after his encounter with Jimmy. Again there is the sense that Sydney is attempting to regain something lost from his past, to find some dignity among the new, young breed of gambler. Sydney loses the bet, but does not change his expression. It is clear that his actions come from a strictly internal place of loneliness and longing. Anderson's point is that when characters avoid confrontations of emotional honesty, the division between the masked self and the true self grows larger.

Sydney's doubleness culminates in the hotel room scene, in which John and Clementine have taken a man hostage for failure to pay for sex. When he shows up, Sydney is cool and composed, but quickly lets his aggression take over. Upon hearing the news that John and Clementine are married, Sydney calls Clementine a hooker, grapples with John and knocks the hostage unconscious. This abrupt change in character is announced when Anderson's camera dollies in for a close-up as Sydney remarks, "This is a pretty...fucked up situation" — his first use of foul language in the film. The film has again given us reason to question Sydney's poised exterior. Anderson does not want to portray Sydney as a sort of superman who can outsmart any situation. Rather, Sydney is shown as being capable of unmitigated hostility. However, we do not judge his actions as malicious, because of his intention to help John and Clementine escape the situation. This is part of Anderson's vision of humanity, in which people do things that we cannot praise nor condemn, but are simply impulsive reactions to a particular moment.

The complexity of Sydney's character goes beyond his own internal emotional struggle and affects his relationships with others. Part of the complexity of his character comes from his implied sexual interest in Clementine. When he brings her back to his hotel room, she sits on the bed while he stands. Anderson frames her face at the level of Sydney's midsection and the shot implies a sort of sexual dominance. (This shot will be repeated in *Magnolia* during the interview between Gwenoviere and Frank.) Clementine asks, "Do you want to fuck me?" Although Sydney declines, it is clear that he longs for intimacy (he says earlier in the film that he is divorced). The next morning, John asks Sydney, "Did you...you know...?" This notion complicates Sydney's role as a father figure for Clementine. As he watches the wedding video of his two surrogate 'children,' Sydney's expression communicates both contentment and jealousy. In John, he sees both a son and sexual rival.

16

But in *Hard Eight*, romantic love is not a perfect proposition. On their wedding night, John slaps Clementine and calls her a "fucking whore." After Sydney sends John and Clementine to safety in Niagara Falls, the couple speaks of getting an annulment. The purest love in the film is not romantic, but familial, between the three central characters. The most sincere expression of love comes in the telephone conversation between Sydney and John, in which Sydney exclaims, "I love you, John, I love you like you were my own son." Anderson clearly desires the film to give us some kind of narrative closure, to solidify the relationship between the characters in the film. This concept is cemented near the end of the film, as Anderson crosscuts between John and Clementine driving across the country and Sydney going to kill Jimmy. As Clementine looks over at John, the film cuts to Sydney in the driver's seat. The film implies the surrogate family is intact, despite the actions necessary to hold it together.

The film's ending, in which Sydney kills Jimmy to keep him silent about the truth of John's father in Atlantic City, reaffirms our inability to judge Sydney's actions as positive or negative. On one hand, he is attempting to protect himself and John from a potentially painful truth, but commits a violent act to achieve it. The characters' decisions in *Hard Eight* are products of ethical choices in which one must justify certain actions for a greater good. In the final shot of the film, Sydney is back in the same coffee shop that began the film.[22] The choice to bookend the film with a scene at Jack's Coffee Shop implies a circularity in the narrative, whereby Sydney will look for a new chance encounter. As he will do in each of his first three films, Anderson desires to impress a lasting image into our minds. In *Hard Eight*, Anderson includes the coda sequence of Sydney killing Jimmy as way to achieve a sense of finality in the film – judgment comes for those characters who we dislike and retribution is given to the protagonists. By ending the film in this manner, Anderson has established his desire to commercialize his work – to give mainstream audiences the resolution that accompanies the bulk of Hollywood filmmaking. This idea would come to its fullest realization in his next film, *Boogie Nights*.

It is my dream to make a film that is true...and right...and dramatic.
—Jack Horner in **Boogie Nights**

CHAPTER 2

BOOGIE NIGHTS (1998): A PORTRAIT OF THE AMERICAN FAMILY

By 1996, *Hard Eight* had been received warmly by critics, but failed to do much at the box office. Yet based on the critical buzz of the film, New Line Cinema President Michael De Luca agreed to give Anderson $15 million to make another film. This project, which was to become *Boogie Nights*, had been an idea that Anderson had developed for several years prior to its release. Growing up in the San Fernando Valley in suburban Los Angeles, Anderson was raised in an area that stood in close proximity to both the world's 'legitimate' filmmaking and pornography capital. But for Anderson, the distinction between the two was not as clear as one might imagine. Instead of viewing X-rated filmmaking as an alternative culture, Anderson saw it as a parallel culture to Hollywood. As a young man in the late 1970s, he became fascinated with the culture of pornography and its appeal to large audiences (*Behind the Green Door*, *Amanda By Night* and *Deep Throat* were all commercial successes at theaters). Nevertheless, the idea of making a film that was socially critical of the entertainment industry was the furthest thing from his mind. For Anderson, the oddity of the family atmosphere of the porn industry is what attracted him to the material.

Boogie Nights began ten years prior to its commercial release as a video project called *The Dirk Diggler Story*, made in 1988 on a VHS camera on location in the San Fernando Valley. The story is centered on an idealistic young actor eager to make it big in the pornography industry. During the 1970s in the Valley, pornography was everywhere, becoming one of the region's major exports. Anderson grew up in an area at a time when porn actors were treated with almost the same respectability as Hollywood stars. Loosely based on the life of real-life porn star John Holmes, *The Dirk Diggler Story* is a narrated account of the rise, fall and eventual death of the title character. When he had a chance to expand the script in the summer of 1995, Anderson was able to extend the narrative to include a large ensemble cast of characters. Producer Daniel Lupi claimed that Anderson was much more demanding about control over *Boogie Nights* after a negative experience with the concessions made during the production of *Hard Eight*. Shooting began in July 1996 and lasted nearly three months. Anderson recalls a relatively easy shoot with virtually no interference from the studio. During editing, the film met some resistance from the MPAA over the removal of some sexually explicit material, but Anderson was able to acquire an R-rating by trimming just forty seconds of footage. After a four-month delay, the film was finally released at the Toronto Film Festival in September 1997.

The goal of the film was to create the feeling of an extended family. Anderson summarizes his film this way: "It's about a lot of people searching for dignity, and trying to find any kind of love and affection they can get. And they find it in really fucked up and twisted ways—but they get it."[23] Before shooting began, Anderson spent several months on the set of real pornographic film shoots. What fascinated him was the cohesion of the actors and the crew as well as the support system involved with such a socially taboo occupation. It was this strange camaraderie that he attempted to foster on his own set. John C. Reilly says, "Paul Thomas Anderson is the type of director who watches an actor as an audience member would. He would run over to me sweating and excited about the scene, offering me minute suggestions about wiping my brow or something. Paul is invested in noticing every detail about an actor's performance."[24]

The most significant way that Anderson facilitated closeness on the set was through careful choices in casting: "I write parts for actors that are my friends or actors that I don't know that I really want to work with."[25] Not only would Anderson cast his friends in his films, but he also wrote parts tailored to each actor's specific idiosyncrasies and would encourage actors to be as natural as possible in their scenes. To accomplish this, he would sometimes ask them to wear what they brought with them instead of changing into costume. To create a natural performance, Anderson sometimes did not tell actors what was supposed to happen in a scene, but instead let them feel out the emotion of the scene naturally without preparation. Regarding his actors, Anderson says, "I treat their characters with the same respect and dignity that I have for real people. My relationship with the actor is right there on-screen."[26] Part of this rapport comes out in the actors' freedom to improvise. One of Anderson's stock actors, Don Cheadle, recalls that *Boogie Nights* was about a quarter unscripted.[27] John C. Reilly recalls footnotes in the shooting script where Anderson had written, "John will keep talking here."[28] Improvisation and freedom were ways to allow the actors to concentrate on emotion rather than focusing on blocking or lines.

The familial feeling on the set was not just a product of Anderson's directorial style, but necessary for the thematic elements of the film. The concept of the family is pivotal in *Boogie Nights*, as well as each of his subsequent films. Anderson's own broken home may have had a lot to do with this need to emotionally explore the family as a source of love, betrayal and abandonment. He freely admits to this idea when discussing the repetition of the family theme in his films: "It's kind of showing all my cards isn't it? Ok, I'm trying to create this little family."[29] Anderson continues, saying that the presence of the surrogate family comes from an issue he was dealing with at the time he made *Boogie Nights*. "It's just a very personal need. I'm applying a very personal need to storytelling…and that's fine. It's the truth."[30] By choosing a deeply personal subject for his film, Anderson actually touches on something quite universal—a need to belong and a sense of community—a need that is fundamental to both Anderson's thematic structure and *modus operandi*.

As Roger Ebert claims about *Boogie Nights*, "This is a film about filmmaking."[31] In fact, Anderson likens his film to a Busby Berkeley backstage musical, which deals with a behind-the-scenes look at the lives in the entertainment industry.[32] More precisely, the narrative structure of *Boogie Nights* covers the years from 1977 until 1984 and follows the relatively standard formula of the 'rise and fall' film. For Anderson, the 1970s represented a Golden Age for both the pornography business and the 'legitimate' cinema, which ended with the coming of video in the 1980s.[33] Anderson says, "In terms of structure and emotion, it was clear: first half/second half, 1970s/1980s."[34] However, this notion severely limits the range of the film. The first half of the film is presented as overwhelmingly positive (despite its seedy subject matter), with everything working out for most of the characters. After the New Year's Eve party, the film swings abruptly to a sharp fall. The danger of bisecting a film into a first half/second half, good times/bad times structure is that actors tend to adhere to this artificial organization. In other words, a script that is segmented in such a way limits the range and subtlety of an actor's performance by dictating which emotions are correct for each half of the film.

In some ways, however, Anderson fights against such a determinate structure. As with *Hard Eight*, Anderson creates a doubleness in his characters to achieve a perpetual frustration of linearity. Most characters in his films either consciously or unconsciously lead double lives. In *Hard Eight*, Sydney's doubleness was purely psychological, as he pretended to be a high-class gambler though he was actually a petty gangster. In *Boogie Nights*, the

20

separation of Eddie's two lives is both physical and psychological. The film portrays Eddie's home life in Torrance with his mother as unloving and abusive, and contrasts that relationship with the welcoming fatherliness of Jack Horner. Eddie's image of himself as an action star conflicts with and eventually replaces his true identity. But the juxtaposition of Eddie's two homes complicates our understanding of his character. On one hand, Anderson shows us one emotional door closing and another opening. However, the world Eddie enters at Jack's house is one of exploitation and emotional dysfunction. Although the atmosphere at Jack's house is accommodating and communal, the film gives us reason to question if this is a positive step for Eddie. The film has presented us with two possible families for Eddie, but neither is a source for unconditional love.

Anderson establishes the idea of the two families through editing. When Eddie's mother throws him out of her house and slams the door behind him, the film cuts directly to the door of Jack's house opening to welcome him. This connection is echoed later as Jack sits quietly smoking and watching Eddie and Rollergirl have sex. Anderson dissolves from Jack's face directly to Eddie's mother sitting in a chair smoking, waiting for Eddie to return. The film suggests that neither of Eddie's families is an adequate source of love. This is central to Anderson's vision of the world, in which one's self-deception leads ultimately to an emotional reckoning when a character is forced to confront his doubleness.

Anderson also uses dialogue to suggest that Jack, Amber, Rollergirl and Eddie make up a sort of nuclear family. When Eddie is introduced to Amber, Jack says, "She's a mother to all those who need love." Likewise, when Rollergirl and Amber use cocaine at Jack's house, Rollergirl desperately pleads, "I want you to be my mother, Amber. I'll ask you if you're my mother and you say, 'yes.' Ok? Are you my mother?" Although Anderson identifies this speech with what he calls 'cocaine talk,' the film is asserting, albeit somewhat ham-fistedly, its desire to link Rollergirl and Amber as a mother and daughter. However, Anderson's tendency is to clarify how we imagine his characters. This desire for clarity results in language that overstates the obvious and confirms what we already suspected about them.

The film seeks to bolster its portrayal of the need for family by showing each character's problems echoed in another character. Amber's work in pornography causes her to lose her son, while Buck loses the loan money for opening his business. Scotty J. tries to imitate Eddie, just as Eddie mimics the action stars he admires. The world of *Boogie Nights* is one in which everyone pretends to be something else. Anderson begins making these linkages in the scenes following the opening nightclub sequence by showing three successive 'coming home' stories (Jack and Amber, Little Bill, and Eddie.) Amber argues with her ex-husband on the phone about seeing her son; Little Bill catches his wife in bed with a younger man; Eddie sneaks back into his house. Anderson's films often bring several characters to the same emotional point at the same time in order to establish a link between their common problems. By editing the film in this way, Anderson wants us to see the different stories as a single, unified narrative and not as the story of several individuals' lives.

The character of Buck Swope (Don Cheadle) is in many ways a character close to the heart of the film's moral lesson about finding love as well as one's identity in a society that discourages individuality. Throughout the film, Anderson frequently shows Buck donning a different outfit in an attempt to find an identity with which he is comfortable. Anderson often plays these moments for comedy, as the absurdity of his persona increases with each clothing change — from a black cowboy to an Egyptian to a rapper. However, there is a genuine sadness in his character; he never feels comfortable in his own shoes. From his troubled career at the stereo store to his inability to get a loan because of his work in pornography, Buck's struggle to find a true self contrasts with Eddie's alter ego, Dirk Diggler.

Whereas the trajectory of Buck's character progresses towards a normal life with a wife and child, Eddie's character moves in the opposite direction. Discontented by his home life, Eddie willfully assumes the nickname of Dirk Diggler in his films. However, the pseudonym soon overtakes his identity. On a shoot, Eddie asks Jack, "I was wondering if you could call me Dirk Diggler from now on." Eddie never doubts his identity and lives in an emotional world of denial, whereas Buck's constant uncertainty facilitates his escape the life of pornography. Anderson compounds the binary of Eddie's two separate lives by adding another level of artifice to his character. As Eddie sinks deeper into self-deception, Anderson creates the role of Brock Landers, a role for the character of Dirk Diggler. Essentially, the film has increased the distance of Eddie from his former life at home—his alias now has an alias. This idea culminates in Eddie's defense of his on-screen persona: "Hey, I'm Dirk Diggler. Brock Landers is just a character I play." The irony, of course, is that he is neither—he is Eddie Adams.

By compounding Eddie's self-deceit, *Boogie Nights* is as much about the American dream as it is about the pornography industry. Anderson's point is to show how American

22

culture requires individuals to simultaneously maintain multiple selves appropriate for different situations. However, Anderson does not condemn his characters because of this quality. He says, "I think they have an emotional honesty, but there's something stripped and raw and childlike about a lot of them."[35] This childlike quality Anderson describes gets to the heart of the film's concern with American culture. Although most characters exhibit a patently American buy-now pay-later attitude in the film, there is the indication that they must ultimately answer for their recklessness. Ultimately, it is the difference between the paths of Dirk and Buck that defines the film's lesson for the viewer—we live in a culture that encourages the pursuit of fantasy. Eddie lives as a child would, in a world without responsibility or consequences, whereas Buck is concerned with financial security and settling down.

In addition to the film's association with the American dream, *Boogie Nights* is also full of allusions to Americana, from the cowboy character Buck plays to the onscreen personas of two of Jack's actors, Chest Rockwell (recalling American painter Norman Rockwell) and Amber Waves (from "America, The Beautiful"). But beyond simple name games, the film presents the problems of this small group of actors as representative of the American desire for material success as well as love and asks if the pursuit of both is possible. The interrelation of sex and money in the pornography industry in *Boogie Nights* points to the deterioration of American business values. Sex is an act of love for Eddie (we see him in bed with his girlfriend Cheryl Lynn) but also a means of commerce and a means of self-deception. As Eddie says, in a line that is overly-wise coming from such a dull-witted character, "Everyone is blessed with One Special Thing." The film does not want to be unequivocal in the declaration of its fundamental moral. By having Eddie say this line (as well as the film's final scene where he talks about guilty feelings), Anderson pulls the viewer out of his character in order to ensure that we understand his larger statement about the individual the context of the family and society.

This notion of the individual using his or her divine gifts to achieve one's destiny is at the heart of the film's take on the American dream. Some characters realize their version of the dream by leaving the pornography industry and starting their lives over in new business ventures. Maurice opens his own nightclub; Reed becomes a professional magician; Buck owns and operates a stereo equipment store and has a child with Jessie St. Clair (Melora Walters). Nevertheless, there is the indication by the film that these dreams are not fully

23

achieved. The sign of Maurice's nightclub misspells his name; Reed's magic act is actually performed in an exotic entertainment club; and Buck is still assuming false identities in the business world (now in the guise of a 1980s rapper). *Boogie Nights* seems to suggest that compromises must always be made, even for the characters that escape the temptation of pornography.

However, for some characters, the American dream means an all-out embrace of material culture. Eddie's bedroom is the center of the film's representation of materialism. On the wall hangs several posters of naked women, one of Al Pacino from *Serpico*, Bruce Lee, and finally, a poster of a red Corvette overlaid with the words "American Dream." The set design of Eddie's bedroom is an externalization of Eddie's fantasies of success. As the camera spins 360°, Eddie is left standing in front of a full-length mirror performing karate, surrounded by the images of his idea of fulfillment. The image Eddie has formed of success consists of sex, drugs, and rock and roll; it is this attitude that the film suggests will ultimately lead to emotional emptiness. For Eddie, materiality replaces the desire for human connection, which the film pinpoints as something wrong with American culture. This idea culminates during Amber's tour of Dirk's house where he has surrounded himself with the objects of his fantasies. Again, Anderson does not want us to miss this point, as Dirk's red Corvette immediately recalls the poster on his bedroom wall.

Still, Anderson is reluctant to admit to the social criticism in his films. Anderson claims, "I'm not really interested in how pornography fits into some universal moral framework. I wanted to explore the society that this little culture creates for itself."[36] For Anderson, the interest of the film lies in human interaction, the personal, the microcosmic. "My first concern was the moral and political and social structure of Jack's fucking house: there's the pool, and the living room and the bedroom, here's the office. That's what the movie is first."[37] Anderson uses Jack's house as the anchor to which all happiness, misery, hope, and despair are tied. It is this place that witnesses the rise of Eddie Adams, his brief stay at the top and his inevitable fall.

The second half of the film, beginning with 1980, follows what Anderson calls the "long way down."[38] Although some characters like Becky Barnett or Buck Swope receive second chances, other characters, such as Rollergirl and Eddie, are not allowed to escape the lifestyle. Juxtaposed to Rollergirl's wild life as a porn actress, Anderson includes several

24

scenes that accentuate her double life—he shows her in a high school classroom or waitressing in a nightclub, but intermingles them with shots of her having casual sex for Jack's camera and doing drugs. As in his other films, Anderson does not allow these worlds to exist independent of each other for long, but instead, merges them in the climax of Rollergirl's subplot. In a porn experiment gone awry, Rollergirl has sex with a random man, who happens to recognize her from high school, which leads to an embarrassing, violent outburst. Her doubleness, as with most characters in the film, is brought together by coincidence and destiny and thrusts her into situations where fate compels her to reach an emotional breaking point.

That is not to say, however, that Anderson's characters always evolve or encounter new understandings during the course of the film. Anderson describes it in the following way:

> Usually what you see in a movie is that the characters become smarter at the end of the movie, somehow. That doesn't really happen here. Everybody is the same. Maybe if there's a change, it's like one degree. Normally you see a 90 degree change in a movie. To me, they're all pretty much the exact same people as they were at the beginning of the movie.[39]

The last half of the film leaves the viewer with an uncertainty whether or not the characters have changed or learned anything from their pain. Anderson says, "I tried to come up with the saddest happy ending I could come up with."[40] This notion ties into the fact that Anderson does not judge his characters, in that he refuses to kill them off (as in an Altman film) or show them ultimately winning out against the system, as in the world of most Hollywood films. Rather, by the end of *Boogie Nights*, some actors continue to make pornography and some go on to other things. Regardless, the film leaves us to question if we have been shown villains or heroes. The answer lies somewhere in the middle—in other words— they are both. They are characters capable of incredible tenderness one moment and unsettling malevolence the next. It is this aspect to Anderson's filmmaking that makes his characters closer to real, complete people. They are neither virtuous nor wicked, but, as in life, make mistakes and often cannot see through their self-delusion.

In one of the final sequences of the film, Dirk and his cohorts go to Rahad Jackson's house for a cocaine buy. It is perhaps the most removed sequence from the narrative structure that *Boogie Nights* establishes. In a technique that originates with Anderson's affinity for Jonathan Demme's *Something Wild*, the course of the film changes tonal directions completely. These shifts occur in what Anderson calls "gearshift movies," where a movie change its focus and feels as if it does not belong with the rest of the film.[41] The bizarre events of the scene (Cosmo repeatedly setting off fireworks and Rahad playing Russian roulette) are disconcerting. This coda ending, like the killing that ends *Hard Eight*, is meant to cement an enduring impression in the viewer's mind. The intensity of the scene, with its gun blasts, firecrackers, Russian roulette, blaring soundtrack of "Sister Christian" and "Jessie's Girl," and exaggerated screaming is meant to overwhelm us with emotion and allow us to enter the frenzied psychology of Dirk.[42]

But the real thrust regarding the peculiarity of the scene comes from the introduction of new characters nearly two hours in the film. The kinetic acting of Todd Parker (whom we have seen before, but only briefly) and Rahad Jackson takes central importance in the sequence, while Eddie, Reed and Scotty assume passive roles in the exchange. This shift in the film's focus is presented in a radically different mode than the rest of the film and gives an unpredictable instability to the scene. The viewer (as well as Eddie) takes on an outsider's perspective and we do not know in what direction the danger lies. Todd and Rahad are not given any redeeming characteristics but are simply victims of their own pathology and drug abuse. The film implies the recklessness of Rahad and Todd as manifestations of the end of the road for Eddie if he continues on the same path of careless behavior. In this way, the sequence functions narratively to bring Eddie to his lowest point morally and provides the catalyst for his need for redemption.

However, the final scene of the film, in which Eddie returns to Jack's house and is given a second chance, is bittersweet at best. The ending of the film presents us with an ambiguous notion of where the main characters have landed emotionally. The scene begins with Jack walking through the house with the same carefree attitude with which he began the film. He ends up in Amber's dressing room, as she gazes blankly at her reflection in the mirror. The film cuts directly from Amber's mirror image to Eddie dressed in full Brock Landers attire. As Eddie stares at his image in the mirror, we are left to wonder if the characters have come full circle with a new understanding or gone nowhere, having resigned themselves to living in a world of self-delusion. Anderson's view of this scene takes a more referential tone: "Mark Wahlberg is playing Eddie Adams pretending to be Dirk Diggler, whose character is Brock Landers, giving the speech by Robert De Niro playing Jake La Motta, who imitates Marlon Brando playing Terry Malloy doing Shakespeare."[43] Although

26

Shakespeare probably never had gargantuan phalluses in mind when he wrote Hamlet, the point is taken. *Boogie Nights'* Eddie Adams comes from a dramatic tradition in which self-deception and denial are the foundations of human suffering. Anderson's film communicates how difficult it is to break this cycle of self-deceit in our culture and that learning from one's mistakes does not always mean emerging from one's problems unscathed. This concept would be a central thesis in Anderson's next film, *Magnolia*.

*Every artist—be it a painter, composer, or filmmaker—
has one song he writes over and over again. And the beautiful
thing about this endeavor is that you don't realize
you're writing the same song repeatedly, but in fact,
it keeps returning to you wearing the same blue gown.*

–Leonard Cohen

*L'amour est un oiseau rebelle / Love is a rebellious bird
Que nul ne peut approvoiser, / that nobody can tame,
Et c'est bien en vain qu'on l'appelle, / and it's all in vain to call it,
S'il lui convient de refuser. / if it chooses to refuse.*

—*from Bizet's* Carmen *and the "What Do
Kids Know?" game show in* Magnolia

CHAPTER 3

MAGNOLIA (1999): CANCER, TELEVISION, AND OTHER DISEASES

When *Boogie Nights*' six-month run at theaters was over, the film had made close to $35 million, which more than doubled its modest $15 million budget. The critical acclaim that surrounded the film was equally impressive and Anderson was catapulted to the status of a *wunderkind*, an up-and-coming independent director. The revival of studio independent filmmaking in the early 1990s had offered little in the way of emotional exploration or an introspective mode of expression.[44] Consequently, Anderson's name was mentioned alongside Robert Altman and Martin Scorsese as a figure who audiences looked to for a different cinematic experience. Consequently, in November 1997, as *Boogie Nights* went into wide release, Anderson set out to capitalize on his success by producing another film quickly. He aimed at making something smaller and more personal, in contrast to the sweeping costume drama that *Boogie Nights* was. Anderson says, "I wanted to make something that was intimate and small-scale, and I thought that I would do it very, very quickly."[45] He began simply with the image of Melora Walters' face and the soundtrack of singer/songwriter Aimee Mann. Anderson remembers the script's development in this way: "It started out as lists of things that are interesting to me — images, words, ideas — and slowly they started resolving themselves into sequences and shots and dialogue."[46] Soon, as Anderson wrote more parts for his friends and stock actors, the script snowballed into a 190-page magnum opus with

28

multiple stories intersecting through cosmic coincidence. Based on the strength of the script and with the reputation garnered from the success of *Boogie Nights*, Anderson was also able to persuade Tom Cruise to work for free. Moreover, New Line Cinema chief Michael De Luca was willing to relinquish total control to Anderson over the film's marketing. Not only did Anderson receive final cut on *Magnolia*, but he also designed the film's poster, the theatrical trailer, the television spots and the DVD release. Principal photography began on January 12, 1999 and was planned at a hundred days, a lengthy shoot even by Hollywood standards. Production was more intense than Anderson's previous projects, due to the larger budget, sprawling script and an almost six-month shooting schedule. The film finally opened on December 8, 1999, nearly two years after Anderson had begun writing the screenplay. But because of its length and reputation for being a "difficult" film for viewers, *Magnolia* failed to connect with commercial audiences and brought in just $22 million in the U.S., just over half of its $37 million budget. Despite failing at the box office, the film won overwhelming critical praise and garnered several awards at international festivals, including winning the Golden Bear at the 2000 Berlin Film Festival.

Magnolia is a film that attempts to resist any compartmentalization. Its narrative loosely follows the lives of nine 'main' characters during one day on Magnolia Boulevard in the San Fernando Valley. *Magnolia* continues Anderson's interest in marginalized characters – what he calls "life's bystanders."[47] They are people who have been damaged by the world, but more importantly, continue to damage themselves. Each of these characters lives in some sort of familial situation that doubles as the source of their misery and the vessel of redemption and forgiveness. In this way, the film inherits this notion from Jack Horner in *Boogie Nights*. The family is presented simultaneously as a necessary agent for finding acceptance and love as well as the single most destructive influence on people's lives.

A sense of connectedness is very important to our conception of each individual's path to emotional understanding. The characters in *Magnolia* are portrayed as sharing common traits with one another while still retaining unique characteristics as individuals. There are no main characters, but rather an evenly balanced examination by the director of several interlocked people with sufficient screen time given to each to develop a feeling of distinctiveness. Despite the individuals' need for one another as well as commitment to a sense of belonging, the film simultaneously sets the individual and the group in opposition to each other.   This concurrent rejection of and dependence on the family generates the conflicts of the film, rendering the group both the cause of and solution to the individuals' problems.   For example, the film juxtaposes Frank T.J. Mackey's troubled family past with his current job as a chauvinistic self-help guru to emphasize the futility of denying one's associations with family.   Mackey's destructive family life has essentially made him what he is, and it is only through his family that he can find a redemptive breakthrough, which he simultaneously relies on and shuns.   This ambivalent relationship with the American family was the foundation for drama in Anderson's first three films and it reaches its pinnacle in *Magnolia*.   Actor William H. Macy describes the characters' problems in the following way:

> [They have] reached the end of what they were doing and they can't do what they were doing anymore.   Everybody's in crisis – they've reached some sort of critical mass.   Everybody is realizing that they've got to start something new.   Everybody wants forgiveness for what they've done, and all of the people are looking for love.[48]

At several points in the film, a character will say, "go, go, go,"[49] as if the lives of each character have been all action and no reflection.   It is as if the morally empty behavior of *Hard Eight* and *Boogie Nights* are being paid for in *Magnolia*.   *Magnolia* does not want to let its characters off as easily as the characters in Anderson's previous films do.   In a way, *Magnolia* is the final chapter in Anderson's trilogy of family films.   Anderson states that *Boogie Nights* was saying, "Just hang out with your friends, it's a lot easier to hang out there than it is to go back home.   [*Magnolia*] is saying, 'Smarten up and go home.'"[50]   In a lyric from Aimee Mann's soundtrack that sums up the film's theme, "It's not going to stop until you wise up."   Making *Magnolia* was not simply a matter of creating fictional characters with extreme emotional problems, but rather, required Anderson to experience a "wising up" process as well.   To an extent, Anderson, like his characters, had been busily going about his career since 1996 without a lot of time for reflection.   Although *Magnolia* was an exhausting production, Anderson found that he was probing for answers as much as his characters were.   "Anybody who's even remotely self-aware is always wondering how to make themselves better, or why they seem to keep making the same mistakes over and over."[51]   *Magnolia* is a film concerned with adult problems.   Anderson reiterates this concept in the following statement:

30

I just reflect a lot upon getting older. And when I will look back some day, I don't want to lie down on the bed like Jason Robards in my film and ask: "What the hell did I do?" I really think that way: I want to be a good human being, I want to make something of my life, I want to be able to say, I did something really great.[52]

This concept is ultimately what the film seeks to portray – new understandings brought about by a day of emotional reckoning. In a sense, this notion of a character's transformation is different from Anderson's previous films. The characters of *Hard Eight* and *Boogie Nights* both end the film where they started (Sydney back in the same coffee shop that began the film, Eddie back at Jack's house doing pornography). These two films suggest that the characters are trapped in a circular pattern of behavior, a recurrent cycle of eternal return. Their transformations are, at best, minimal; however, in *Magnolia*, Anderson suggests that a return to old patterns is no longer sufficient. *Magnolia* does not allow individuals any possibility of circumventing their problems. Macy sees this as a cultural metaphor for the end of the 20th century – "We can't do in the next hundred years what we've done in the last hundred. We won't survive. We must do something different – we all know it."[53]

What Macy is describing is a sense of the apocalyptic mood that the film conveys. Released just one month prior to the millennium, the film embodies the spirit of many of the films of the late 1960s and early 1970s – a spirit which sought to call an end to a certain way of thinking in America and to find new patterns of behavior. It is hard to deny that Anderson's film, with its inclement weather and its rainstorm of frogs, embodies the same tone of urgency that the films of Robert Altman or Jean-Luc Godard do. However, *Magnolia* does not convey the level of cynicism of an Altman or Godard film, in which elements of fate and capriciousness are used against humanity, rather than in service of it.[54] Anderson's film does not echo the fatalism of Peter Fonda's "we blew it" at the conclusion of *Easy Rider*. The disparity between *Magnolia* and these films is best expressed in terms the characters' reaction to this urgency – the chance to do away with old systems of social control, rather than a resignation to the institutions that force us into certain destructive patterns. *Magnolia* shuns this cynicism and is ultimately a celebratory vision of life. Anderson adds that "making cynical movies is easy, it's lazy. It allows you not to go deeply into it."[55] *Magnolia* upholds the possibility for an escape from emotional annihilation in the pre-September 11th prosperity of the late 1990s.

31

Nevertheless, *Magnolia*'s celebration of life is somewhat difficult to discern because the film takes itself very seriously. Unlike *Hard Eight* or *Boogie Nights*, *Magnolia* uses comedy very sparsely and rarely with the tongue-in-cheek playfulness of Dirk Diggler or John Finnegan.[56] Rather, the film's comedy occurs when a character unconsciously acts within a predetermined system. For instance, when Dixon pretends to be a rapper and Jim Kurring calls him "Coolio" or "Ice-T," the comedy comes only partially from the absurdity of the dialogue. We laugh because of the discrepancy between Dixon's playfulness and Jim's condescension, at Jim "playing cop" with a young black male. Likewise, when Jim gathers confidence to tell Claudia that he lost his gun, the moment plays both comically and seriously. The triviality of his anxiety is funny, but the emotional importance he has placed on his gun also makes us sympathize with him. Similarly, Frank T.J. Mackey's comic moments occur when he is playing a role. The "respect the cock and tame the cunt" speeches are humorous not because of their vulgarity, but because of Frank's *unawareness* of their vulgarity. Each comical moment is compromised by an element of sadness for the character's inability to recognize the role he or she is playing.

These pretenses extend a central Andersonian thesis that runs through each of his films. Many of the characters in *Magnolia* maintain a surface persona while suppressing the vulnerable parts of their identity. As in life, everyone has something to hide. The drama of the film is based on our understanding of the chasm existing between the true self and the phony self. Essentially, the film sets these two directions of each character in motion, with the gap between them widening in every scene. In order to dispose of any doubt that these two selves exist for each character, Anderson's screenplay makes this gap as defined as possible. Frank keeps up an image as a lady-killer while concealing his feelings of betrayal and abandonment by his parents. Quiz kids Donnie Smith and Stanley Spector are admired for their intelligence but only want the reciprocity of affection from their families. Jimmy Gator is a successful entertainer but also molests his daughter and cheats on his wife. Anderson's film teaches us that the only way to move forward is by a direct confrontation with the mistakes of our past, and that this confrontation has far-reaching consequences beyond ourselves, affecting those who are connected to us.

Magnolia dramatically connects all of the characters through the themes of love, regret, redemption and forgiveness, connections that are created by the film's editing. The prologue of the film shows three separate historical events, each containing an unbelievable series of coincidences. The narrator takes us through the three events of chance that are disconnected from the main narrative as well as from each other. This opens the film to explore its themes irrespective of being tied to a singular narrative. Similarly, the first third of the film shows us various disconnected lives, jumping from one character to another. Our experience of the film is initially a gathering of information about the characters, i.e. Jim Kurring is a straight-laced police officer, Claudia Wilson is a cocaine addict, Jimmy Gator is a game show host, etc. At first, our introductions to these characters are unrelated but are simply united by a common loneliness or void needing to be filled. Jim is introduced to us through a personal dating service announcement, Claudia goes home from bars with strangers, and Stanley is manipulated by his father who uses his son's intelligence for money. However, as the film progresses into its second hour, we begin to learn about the interrelations and conflicts of the characters, i.e. the tension between Jimmy and Claudia, the estrangement of Frank and Earl, and the sham marriage of Earl and Linda.

Although the film encompasses the lives of such a large group, it is the sense of the individuals' one-on-one relationships that matter the most in the film. The film works this notion into its editing structure, consisting almost exclusively of an endless series of one-on-one interactions for the entire middle third of the film. One advantage of using a crosscutting technique is to control the emotional status of each character at any given time. However, Anderson's adherence to the film's structural decision of keeping everyone at the same emotional state can sometimes ring untrue. When Jim loses his gun, his reaction feels overstated to a viewer who has just heard about molestation and child abandonment from other characters.[57] Although Jim clearly attaches emotional meaning to his job as a police officer, the film is unable to bring him gradually to the same level of despair as the other characters. Thus, this function is carried out by the contrivance of losing his gun. A similar device brings Linda to her breakdown point in the pharmacy. The young clerk's words ("You must have a lot going on in your life for all that stuff there...what exactly do you have wrong, you need all this stuff?") are far-fetched and serve only to incite a violent outburst in Linda's character. Similarly, to bring Stanley to an emotional breaking point, the film exaggerates his father's abusiveness. When his father speaks with other parents at the game show, he says, "You have to be subtly abusive so they don't know what's going on." The problem with this type of characterization is that it reduces people to ideas. In life, the truth is that people often do not see or deny their abusive behavior. Because the film makes Stanley's father's mistreatment of his son a conscious act, the father is one-dimensional and functions solely as a catalyst for Stanley's assertiveness near the end of the film, but ceases to have any conflict or inner turmoil himself.

Another way the film progresses is the establishment of a central point of convergence for the characters—the "What Do Kids Know?" game show.[58] As with Jack's house in *Boogie Nights*, every character, in some capacity, is connected to this anchor in the film's development. The game show is the quintessence of artifice, the epitome of the creation of a false world. It is here that Anderson allows the external and secret lives to collide. At a key emotional moment in the game show sequence, Stanley refuses to be an instrument of his father's greed and demands to be loved on live television. Jimmy Gator, the show's host, is also exposed for having molested his daughter. Earl Partridge, the producer, regrets his sullied relationships with his ex-wife and his son on his deathbed. The television camera of Anderson's game show probes the inner sanctums of their personal secrets and provides only one path forward through an emotional collapse and rebuilding.

However, the idea of connecting each of the stories through relation to the game show is actually a limiting feature of the film. Since the prologue, we have not been given instances of coincidence or fate, but have simply been presented with the complexities of each individual and their immediate worlds. But the film does not remain in this mode. Instead, Anderson intertwines their narratives, an idea that works against itself by establishing a sort of puzzle to be decoded, which amounts to little more than cleverness by the director. By establishing linkages between the network of characters, the film presents a scenario in which the problems of the characters are exceptional to 'those kind of people.' These characters – the sex guru, the cocaine addict, the millionaire producer and the boy genius – are not us. Anderson says that when a writer creates characters, "for the most part, you're writing what you are, but the other half of what you write is the kind of person what you want to be."[59] But by interconnecting their problems through physical relation rather than by mere common humanity, the film unintentionally isolates their problems as being due only to the exceptionality of their existences.

Magnolia's characters are products of what they *believe* they are expressing and are caught living lies. For example, Anderson brings Frank Mackey's inner and outer lives together in an emotional scene between Frank and his interviewer, Gwenovier. In a relentless pursuit of the facts of Frank's past, she exposes his masked pain regarding the

34

truth about his mother and father. Anderson has prepared the viewer to monitor Frank's emotional transformation, which will culminate in the final exchange with his dying father. This breaking point with Gwenovier marks a pivotal moment in both Frank's story as well as the larger narrative involving the rest of the film's characters. It is at this point when Anderson places all of his characters at a crossroads, cutting between the dramatic climaxes of each story. Claudia, a victim of child molestation and a cocaine addict, decides to date Jim the prudish police officer. Donnie Smith professes his love for Brad the bartender. Linda Partridge admits to her infidelities and accepts the approaching death of her husband. In all of these instances, the first half of the film has shown the widening gap between the real and artificial personas of these characters. But it is in the climactic second hour that the gap is closed, culminating in each character's emotional breakthrough and new ways of understanding. By editing each story's climactic sequence together into the second hour of the film, Anderson has linked the characters through a common problem—their inability to confront their interior lives.

Despite its broad scope, the film is deceptively linear. In fact, *Magnolia* belongs to an extremely conventional mode of storytelling in American film that began with D.W. Griffith's *Intolerance*.[60] The "What Do Kids Know?" game show functions not only as the central point of connection for the film's intertwining narratives, but also serves as a metronome for the film's tempo. For instance, after the initial conflicts for each narrative are set, Jimmy Gator announces, "End of Round One." The result is that one individual's story continues where the last story ends, playing out in a series of transitions that hold the film together as an organic whole. This is a much more insightful and effective method of linking the characters than through the actual biology (Frank and Earl, Jimmy Gator and Claudia), romantic relationships (Jim Kurring and Claudia, Linda and Earl) or acquaintance (Jimmy Gator and Stanley, Phil and Frank). Likewise, the development of the game show corresponds to the emotional battle going on between the children and the adults in the rest of the film. Thus, when Jimmy checks the scores ("the adults are way up with 4775, but that doesn't mean that the game is out of reach for the kids"), the viewer understands that the scores are an indicator that the parents in the film are "winning" the game of control over their children. By editing the film in such a way where the film moves forward narratively based on shared human experiences rather than a puzzle-piece system of interconnecting relationships, *Magnolia* opens up and is able to address a much wider context than simply the lives of a closed circle of flawed people living on the same street.

Magnolia exemplifies what film theorist Leo Braudy calls an "open film."[61] In the open film, we are not shown ourselves but rather a new perspective on our world – it is a film that places us into a context that we can understand emotionally, but one that is not a mirrored reflection of our feelings. Anderson locates the desire to open his film as a reaction against most Hollywood cinema, where one sees "a lot of movies where you can't relate to the ticking bomb going off in the warehouse. How can I emotionally connect to someone who's trying to dismantle the red wire or the blue wire?"[62] Instead, *Magnolia* introduces concepts with which we are categorically familiar – parental abandonment, insecurity in dating relationships, and self-denial – but in a way that is one step removed from our reality and fosters an investigation of more questions and more answers. As actor Philip Seymour Hoffman said in an interview about *Magnolia*, the film expresses "the idea that every minute of your life is completely unknowable.   You can't understand what's going on, ever.   If you start to understand it, there'll be another question. Life is that amazing. Life is that gray. Life is that un-understandable."[63] Part of this lack of foresight comes from a very true-to-life place for Anderson. He agrees with Hoffman: "It's very important if you bring up a topic to make sure that you have a point of view. But also, within that, you can say, 'I'm confused as hell, and I don't have the answers. I'm looking for them just like everybody else.'"[64] Anderson's point is that if a film summarily answers all of its questions, the viewer is left is a state of passivity where the complexity of the film is oversimplified.

One of the ways that the film achieves "openness" is through Robert Elswit's camera movement. For most of the prologue and introductory sequences of the film, the Steadicam moves rapidly through scenes (Stanley's house as he goes to school, Linda as she talks to her doctors on the phone, Phil arriving at Earl's house), exaggerating the intensity of each situation. In addition, the camera has a roaming, searching quality. It follows characters around corners and through long passages (the "What Do Kids Know?" backstage and through Stanley's house). Beyond the simple analogy of characters that are constantly on the move, probing for answers (as with the camera in *Taxi Driver*), the camera takes on an outsider perspective. The camera is not in our position (as in a Hitchcock film) or in the character's subjectivity (as in a Lang film), but rather searches frantically for something on which it can settle. However, as the film moves forward in the final hour, the tempo of the editing slows down to static two-shots as the camera forces our gaze at a particular image for an excruciating duration (Frank's vacant stare during the interview with Gwenovier or Earl's monologue about regret). It is as if the camera assumes a level of sensitivity and compassion – lovingly lingering on faces of people it deems most in need of it.

The camera's intense concentration on each character in the final hour, as in Frank's breakdown on his father's bedside or Donnie's profession of love to Brad the Bartender, brings the film to almost a complete cinematographic standstill at the "Save Me" singing sequence. Although many journalists criticized the scene for breaking the "reality" of the drama, that is exactly the strength of the sequence. In the closed film, Braudy continues, "any self-conscious reference to filmmaking itself would destroy the illusion of sufficiency, [the] feeling that there is no other world."[65] Shattering the illusion of melodrama is the triumph of the scene rather than its hindrance. This occurs numerous times throughout the film beginning with the prologue, in which a chalk diagram is drawn to show a character jumping from a rooftop. The film's self-reflexivity is revisited when Phil calls the operator "Seduce and Destroy" and delivers the following speech:

> I know this all seems silly. I know that maybe I sound ridiculous, like maybe this is the scene of the movie where the guy is trying to get a hold of the long-lost son, but this is that scene. Y'know? I think they have those scenes in movies because they're true, because they really happen. And you gotta believe me: This is *really happening*...See this is the scene of the movie where you help me out.

All of these moments are meant to draw us away from the "reality" of the drama. Anderson is very clearly defining his film in these moments. They are meant to loudly declare that we are watching a film and not a depiction of real lives. A work of art is a failure if it simply presents us with a mirror. In watching Anderson's films, identification can bring the viewer to a dangerous place. If art looks too much like life, then it ceases to be representational or emblematic of something larger than itself. *Magnolia* uses an introspective strategy to attempt to get at something deeper than mere reflection and teach us something about ourselves.

The "Save Me" sequence in *Magnolia* also illuminates an aspect of Anderson's filmmaking since *Hard Eight* – the use of music. To be sure, *Magnolia* is a quintessential melodrama (from the Latin meaning "musical drama") with virtually nonstop music for the middle third of the film. In fact for Anderson, the music comes before the idea: "Music is an essential element of filmmaking. It isn't tacked on, superfluous, or decorative. It gives a life to the image and the emotions."[66] He continues by adding that the soundtrack is as important to a film as the actors and that music was the starting point for the conception of *Magnolia*. While piecing together the different narratives that would eventually be the film's script, Anderson listened incessantly to the songs of Aimee Mann whose lyrics he quotes in the film's dialogue ("Now that I've met you, would you object to never seeing me again?"). Another instance where the music reflects the emotion of the character is Quiz Kid Donnie Smith listening to the song "Dreams." On several occasions, the lyrics coming from Donnie's stereo sing, "Dreams can come true...I can't deny my feelings because they are true." These lines mimic Donnie's constant assertions that he will make his dreams come true. In another instance, we hear the lyrics from the same tune sing "got to say how I feel" directly after Jim and Claudia agree to only say the things that they feel and not lie. By correlating the film's narrative with the lyrics on the soundtrack, Anderson wants to present the characters' problems as being tapped into something more universal, a cultural *Zeitgeist* of feeling in the late 1990s that change is needed.[67] Nevertheless, the rhythmic score and quick cutting are used as a propulsion device in the film, creating drama where there otherwise would be none. In a sense, Anderson is using a delaying technique to keep us in suspense as to whether Frank will connect to Phil on the phone.

This quality of the film's orchestration reverses itself in the final section of *Magnolia*, slowing the pace of the editing. In the film's exposition, the franticness of the camerawork and editing communicated the anxiousness of the characters' inner emotional states. However, as each character is thrust into a breakdown during the second and third hour, the music replaces the pacing as the manner of expressing the intensity of the characters' emotions. As Anderson says, the music "gives the film rhythm, accelerating and slowing the film down."[68] The film's initial frenzied pace followed by a gradual slowing synthesizes in the final sequence with the rain of frogs. As William H. Macy implied, each character has been involved with things that they must ultimately recognize and stop. As the downpour of frogs occurs, the film literally slows to a halt in Stanley's library as he says, "This happens. This is something that happens." As the film moves to slow motion, we have entered a kind of mental space. In fact, the cataclysmic nature of the scene should be read as somewhere between reality and unreality. Anderson chose the rain of frogs because of a story actor Philip Baker Hall told him about witnessing such an event in World War II in Italy. The truth of such an unbelievable occurrence echoes the amazing coincidences of the film's prologue.

However, the frogs also bring an element of fantasy to the sequence. In a film that, since the prologue, has been bound to a depiction of believable occurrences, this scene brings the problems of the characters to a place of cosmic importance. It is not an apocalypse of destruction and judgment as in *Easy Rider* or *Dr. Strangelove*. Rather, the final image of Claudia's smile indicates some degree of positivity and hope that blossoms after the emotional annihilation of the film's painful moments and that the rebuilding process has begun. Anderson does not want to leave us with a chaotic, unresolved ending like Altman's *Nashville*. Essentially, Anderson lets us off the hook for enduring an emotionally depleting experience for three hours. He reaches a compromise by allowing us the sense that the film is unresolved (Jimmy Gator is left in a burning house, we do not know if Claudia will rehabilitate, etc.). Still, the quick smile is enough to allow the viewer to leave the film feeling that all has been set right again, or that it will work itself out in the end.

Love, that is all I asked, a little love, daily, twice daily,
fifty years of twice daily love.

—Samuel Beckett, 1958
Mrs. Rooney in "All That Fall"

Not to sink under being man and wife,
But get some color and music out of life?

—Robert Frost, 1928
"The Investment"

CHAPTER 4

PUNCH-DRUNK LOVE (2002): NEW AVENUES

After the exhausting process of making *Magnolia* in 1999, Anderson needed a break from filmmaking. He decided to get some distance from his own work for about a year and eventually began his next project in 2001. The challenge was accepting the restrictions as well as the possibilities of a 90-minute film. Likewise, coming after a film that touched on death, child abuse and cancer, a romantic comedy seemed the least likely next step for a director who had been hailed as the new hope for America's art filmmaking. These were issues that Anderson was conscious of when he decided to go ahead with the project that would become *Punch-Drunk Love*. It would turn out to be an exercise in brevity and in simplicity, qualities that Anderson was not known for. Two years prior, he had failed to limit *Magnolia* to the small, intimate work he had intended, resulting in being the longest and most arduous production of his career. As always, when Anderson began working on the script, he was writing with specific actors' abilities and limitations in mind. Since the early 1990s, Anderson had admired Adam Sandler's comic ability in both his television and film work. He was equally impressed with Emily Watson's performance in Lars von Trier's *Breaking the Waves*. But as filming began, Anderson was afraid he had made a huge mistake and was not sure he was going to be able to pull off a romantic comedy. About two weeks into production, the cast was not connecting emotionally during takes. But taking a cinematic risk was the goal of the project for Anderson, who frames it this way: "If I did *Magnolia* again, everybody would be, 'So when are you going to do something different?' You have to keep it fresh, keep doing other things. New things, new paths."[69] Filming finally wrapped on March

40

2001 and was premiered about a year later at the 2002 Cannes Film Festival. Although Anderson won Best Director at the Festival for the film, *Punch-Drunk Love* failed commercially in the United States, making only about $17 million.

Anderson always maintains a close relationship with his actors in order to ensure that their performances appeared natural. On the set of *Punch-Drunk Love*, Anderson used the smallest crew he could (fewer than ten people) to make the production as unobtrusive as possible.[70] This was a critical directorial decision, because most of the people appearing in the film were not professional actors. In fact, only Sandler, Watson, Luis Guzman, Philip Seymour Hoffman and Mary Lynn Rajskub were professional actors. The remainder of the cast was comprised entirely of non-professionals. Anderson says, "I like working with real people. They can make your life a lot easier and more comfortable sometimes. They can be more fun to be around sometimes, and actually better at being they are."[71] The four blonde ruffians are actual brothers and five of Barry's sisters in the film are related.[72] For Anderson, working with a familiar, close-knit cast is a method of ensuring that the barriers that often exist between actor and director are minimized – an approach that Anderson had maintained since his earliest short films.

Punch-Drunk Love essentially follows the basic formula of a romantic comedy – lonely boy meets lonely girl and the two fall in love. As in each of Anderson's films, the protagonists are outsiders. Barry and Lena are lonely, confused and emotionally hungry individuals. However, the family theme that has dominated Anderson's work to this point is conspicuously absent. Instead, *Punch-Drunk Love* focuses its narrative explicitly on the characters of Barry and Lena. The concept of concentrating on two people was a challenge for a writer who had been so accustomed to working with large casts. Anderson says, "I think it's harder to make a story about one person because you can't keep cutting to another story. I found that really challenging."[73] Both *Boogie Nights* and *Magnolia* were films that cut away from one story immediately after a scene reached its dramatic climax, rather than following each narrative to its conclusion. Anderson's impulse in these films was to ease the emotional weightiness of each sequence by simply jumping to another story.[74] Although *Punch-Drunk Love* shows an effort to resist this temptation, Anderson finds new ways in which to keep us from indulging in the sentimentalized romance of the characters.

The use of dialogue in the film is the primary way in which Anderson cuts against over-romanticizing. For instance, in a particular exchange between Barry and Lena, Barry says,

"I'm looking at your face and I just want to smash it. I just want to fucking smash it with a sledgehammer and squeeze you're so pretty." Lena replies, "I want to chew your face and I want to scoop out your eyes and eat them and chew them and suck on them." Despite the abnormal and decidedly unromantic nature of this exchange, the film plays it for tenderness and humor. Anderson is attempting to present a view of love wherein such over-the-top dialogue actually functions as an expression of intense devotion, rather than violence or intimidation.[75] By allowing characters to speak in such an unconventional style, the film grants itself a license to present eccentricity as simply part of the world of the film, which we accept. However, the outcome of this anti-romantic style yields the same emotional result as the traditional view of love on film and ultimately upholds the notion of finding one person who truly understands us, no matter how bizarre the means of achieving it. Essentially, *Punch-Drunk Love* still conveys a feeling of idealism and destiny, but presents it in a way more palatable to younger, more cynical audiences by concurrently seeking to distance us from the characters while still allowing us to feel empathy and compassion for them.

However, the film is not simply our empathetic journey with two people struggling to understand one another, but also addresses an American culture that disregards feelings and suppresses the pursuit of emotional connection. Anderson's films are about allowing the human spirit to be opened to experiences that, although painful, prove to lead to new paths of emotional understanding. They are people who are trapped by the impersonality of the world. *Punch-Drunk Love* establishes this notion with the first shot of the film, which shows Barry at a desk in an empty warehouse with bland walls. Anderson's camera stays back from the action, remaining in master shot and emphasizing Barry's separation from any human contact. Barry lives in a vacuum world, a world of emptiness. Apartment buildings are desolate, labyrinthine, monochrome and depersonalizing. Likewise, when Barry walks outside, the Los Angeles streets are void and colorless. The fluorescent lights of the supermarket are blindingly intense and the products are arranged in perfect order. Anderson imagines a world where everything has been processed and pre-packaged for people. Thus, the subsequent car crash and appearance of the harmonium shatters this dullness and indicates that the film will explore the concept of breaking out of a world of sameness. Thus, when Barry travels to Hawaii to meet Lena, the world appears to be less geometric and less controlling as the camera is free to wander through the chaotic streets during a parade or through the audience at a beach concert. In a sense, the world Anderson creates is not our

42

world. The world of *Punch-Drunk Love* has one foot in our world and one foot in the cartoon world. At one point when Barry runs from the Mormon brothers, Anderson shoots his shadow running against the wall, evoking a Dick Tracy-esque level of fictionalization. Likewise, the concept of a man with seven sisters running from four brothers suggests a sort of fairy tale quality to the film. Although these moments play either for comedy or oddness, they drastically alter our relationship to the film. In other words, if the film stayed entirely within the parameters of plausibility, this would be a radically different film and one that is much sadder and desperate than *Punch-Drunk Love*. By removing the audience from a place of believability to one that can indulge in whimsical sequences, the film is lightening the emotional intensity of the audience's relationship with the characters. As with the prologue and epilogue of *Magnolia*, this quality calls attention to the fact that we are watching a film and that we are not to believe everything we see.

In all of Anderson's previous films, the world of the characters existed halfway between the familiar and the strange – the casino floor, the pornography shoot, behind the scenes of a game show – that are not mirrors of our lives, but something akin to it that we accept as realistic. In *Punch-Drunk Love*, we accept the eccentricities by these characters – the pudding/frequent flyer scam, Barry's overstated uncontrollable temper, or the fact that he has seven sisters – and do not judge them as unrealistic or unbelievable. (In fact, all of these three examples are constructed from real accounts that Anderson researched while writing the film.) However, *Punch-Drunk Love* goes further to places that are removed from our concept of reality. The random dropping of the harmonium in the streets or Barry carrying a telephone from Los Angeles to Utah are moments cannot be read as realistic, but demand to be read as figurative.

However, at other moments, the film asks us to invest our deepest emotional connection to the characters' loneliness and subsequent courting process. At Rhonda's birthday party, Barry breaks down while asking his brother-in-law dentist for help with his crying problem and his low self-esteem. Likewise, when Barry is at the restaurant with Lena, she mentions his sister's description of his uncontrollable temper. These scenes demand that we feel a genuine sympathy for Barry's condition as a fleshed-out human being. The film's ambivalent attitude toward making us feel genuine compassion for the characters and seeing them as cartoon characters is a level in which the film frustrates the viewer's desire to know how the film wants them to feel.

43

Part of the cartoonish quality of the film comes from the film's vivid color. In *Punch-Drunk Love*, Anderson uses costuming to contrast with the blandness of the characters' environment. Barry's decision to wear a blue suit to work one day suggests that he has not only chosen to break with old habits, but also that he wishes to reclaim some sense of individuality in his world (his co-workers at the plunger warehouse as well as the auto mechanics next door dress in a uniformed, depersonalized manner). Likewise, Lena dresses in bright red outfits or gleaming white dresses, indicating that these are two characters that the film desires to be foregrounded against the drab world. The film's abrupt transition from the bleak, gray world to a blown-out explosion of color coincides with the emergence of Lena. The culmination of the film's use of color is Jeremy Blake's psychedelic swirls of light that interrupt dialogue mid-sentence. Anderson's technique externalizes Barry's emotional transition – his environment changes and the same streets are now vibrant and pulsating with life and color. When Lena and Barry go to Hawaii, the world appears full of humanness again. But again, Anderson does not allow us to indulge in the scene's sentimentality even at this point in the film. In the tracking shot through the beach at Waikiki, Barry can only muster the comment "It really looks like Hawaii here." In other words, he cannot separate the natural beauty of the scenery from the postcard version of Hawaii that he had envisioned. Like the bright colors of the products in the supermarket, Hawaii is just a commodity in Barry's world, an item that has been packaged for him like the items in the 99¢ Store. In this respect, the film is somewhat ambiguous as to the measure of Barry's transformation. After he falls in love with Lena, Barry is still prone to violent acts (his beating of the four brothers with a crowbar, his ransacking of the restaurant bathroom) and insensitivity (he leaves her at the hospital after the car accident). Nevertheless, this less-than-perfect romance corresponds with Anderson's desire not to over-sentimentalize his movies and we do not judge Barry negatively for his actions.

In terms of Anderson's visual sensibility, *Punch-Drunk Love*'s desire to set people apart with color in a world of monotony resembles the works of French comic Jacques Tati — *Playtime* and *Mon Oncle*. Tati's childlike zaniness is contrasted to nearly everyone in the film and his films are ultimately a colorful celebration of life, expressed by his desire to be different. In fact, Anderson admits to the influence: "I was just in a real love affair with Jacques Tati's movies [during the production of *Punch-Drunk Love*]."[76] The presence of influence is something that Anderson has had to fight with each of his films. While some accused him of being a rip-off artist, others saw him as merely updating the American art film of previous generations for the late 1990s. Anderson says of *Punch-Drunk Love*: "This one came from my stomach. It's referenceless. When you start out, you latch onto other movies, other styles, to help you get across what you're trying to say. But this one is mine somehow – all mine – and I'm proud of that."[77] This statement may be wishful thinking on Anderson's part, as he mentions not only the Tati influence in interviews, but also cites numerous other films as being integral to the process of making the film. Anderson admittedly "borrowed" the scene of Barry's knuckles spelling 'Love' from Robert Mitchum's character in *Night of the Hunter*, as well as numerous Gene Kelly films for the film's sense of music and color. Even Barry's blue suit was a nod to MGM musicals: "It's from *The Bandwagon*, the Vincent Minnelli musical...and if you watch *Singin' In the Rain*, it's sort of indicative of these movies that there's a fantastic blue suit in just about every one of them."[78]

The truth is that many of the filmmakers of Anderson's generation have internalized the films they admire to the point of not recognizing their manifestations in their own work. Beyond the sense that the film was something Anderson could claim as his own, the style of the film also marks a shift in his *oeuvre*. Compared with Anderson's previous three films, Robert Elswit's cinematography is much more raw and loose. In *Magnolia*, Anderson's camera movement was graceful and smooth even during chaotic Steadicam sequences. However, in *Punch-Drunk Love*, Anderson often uses a jerky handheld style. For instance, as Anderson follows Barry around his apartment as he talks to the phone sex operator, the camera tracks him in an almost *verité* style. Likewise, many scenes of Barry at work in the warehouse show a freeform in camerawork, unconcerned with smooth tracks or steady dollies. The effect of such shots is that they are made to appear more realistic, as if we are in the room with Barry. This decision indicates that Anderson clearly wants us to identify with the protagonist and experience his pain from an inside perspective rather than from an observer's standpoint. However, at times, Anderson removes us from getting close to the characters by returning to moments of cinematographic bravado. When Barry and Lena are on Waikiki Beach in Hawaii, Anderson's camera glides seamlessly through the crowd to find them alone at a table.[79] Anderson's visual style is one of precision and aesthetic pleasure. Although this change in style between the Los Angeles and Hawaii scenes may be read as a shift from chaos to harmony in Barry's life, the visually stimulating shots in Hawaii indicate Anderson's desire to allow the audience to get swept up by the film's romance and to show us a world that exists only in the movies.

Superficially, the film creates a world that appears to look like ours. However, the film shows us that the world of these characters is a representational space – an externalization of their trapped feelings. In terms of construction of space, Anderson's visual imagination often approaches the films of Hitchcock. In a Hitchcock film, the character's internal ego alters the external.[80] If a character feels trapped emotionally, he is placed within a milieu of barriers and mazelike hallways.[81] In *Punch-Drunk Love*, Anderson has created an enclosed, limiting space in which the characters interact. This is a concept that has appeared in each of Anderson's feature films. The milieu of each film is a confined space – the casino in *Hard Eight*, Jack's house and the nightclub in *Boogie Nights*, the quiz show in *Magnolia* – that limits the characters' range of motion. They are worlds with specific codes of behavior that, once broken, shatter the pretenses that define it (the poise of the gambler, the legitimacy of the pornographer, the glitziness of the game show). Instead of the traditional Hollywood setup of cartoonish characters in a real location, Anderson's films present almost the direct opposite. These are people with real emotions and real problems who live in an artificially constructed environment.

He achieves this idea by the way he frames many of the shots in the film. An overwhelming number of scenes are framed by enclosures – hallways, alleys, stairways, etc. In *Punch-Drunk Love*, Anderson often shoots even the most ordinary scene using framing devices within the shot. When Georgia threatens Barry the morning after their initial conversation, Anderson keeps Barry in master shot down a hallway in his apartment. Likewise, the film frames the corridors of Lena's apartment building as never-ending and dehumanizing, dwarfing Barry as he tries to find her room. By shooting these scenes in telephoto, Anderson not only flattens the image and lengthens the appearance of the hallway, but also emphasizes the number of "Exit" signs that hang over each doorway. The world of *Punch-Drunk Love* is constantly seeking to impose order onto the chaos of life through various methods of social control. The use of this framing technique visually reinforces what the narrative has already taught us – that people are unconsciously conditioned to follow a clear path dictated to them by social and institutional conventions. As with Eddie Adams' bedroom décor in *Boogie Nights*, this notion speaks to the film's vision of the American dream. From the cavernous warehouse where Barry works to Lena's apartment to supermarkets, the film presents us with innumerable locations that dehumanize us by forcing us to accept uniformity.

As significant as the film's departure from traditional cinematography and dialogue is Anderson's deviation from traditional lighting setups. The contrasts of light and dark are extreme in *Punch-Drunk Love*, changing from near blackness to blinding white within a brief scene. When Barry brings the harmonium inside and begins to play it alone in the dark, the calmness of the scene is shattered by a flood of light from the opening of the warehouse door. Likewise, after Barry's conversation about uncontrollable crying with Walter in a dark room, the film cuts to a brilliantly white supermarket. These shocking juxtapositions of light and dark illustrate a structural objective of the film – to pull us away from a scene when we get too comfortable. Anderson uses not only the contrasts of light and dark, but also loud and soft. Several times in the film, we are lulled by a scene's stillness, only to have the silence violently interrupted a second later. For instance, in one of the opening scenes of the film, the camera peers down a long stretch of highway at twilight. Suddenly, a car unexpectedly flips over and crashes in the street in front of Barry. Later in the film, a family dinner is abruptly ruined by Barry breaking three windows in the house. These moments in the film are meant as a tool to keep us alert and get us to a point where we never know when the next unexpected event will occur. They function in the same manner as the firecracker sequence in *Boogie Nights*, in which the audience's tension arises from not knowing from where to expect danger. These moments also serve to break away from the drama of a particular scene, a typically Andersonian impulse to pull us away from the action before we get to close to a scene. They are a sort of motor for the film, occasionally jarring the viewer to keep us interested in what follows.[82] In *Punch-Drunk Love*, there are no five-minute monologues like the regret speech by Earl Partridge in *Magnolia*. In this respect, Anderson falls short of his stated intention to focus only on the characters without the temptation to cut away, as these abrupt changes serve the same purpose of driving the film forward.

The music in *Punch-Drunk Love* also contributes to our reading of the characters' emotions. Anderson says, "For *Punch-Drunk Love*, I wanted something abrasive, percussive, mixed with lush, good old-fashioned romantic Hawaiian stuff."[83] As with *Magnolia*, the film feels as much driven by the music as by the characters. Anderson adds, "I think movies are fifty percent seeing and fifty percent hearing, and if you don't have one, you're shortchanging the audience."[84] Anderson is not simply referring to the entertainment value provided by a film's scoring, but rather its contribution to the emotions of the characters onscreen. The soundtrack serves two major functions in *Punch-Drunk Love*; first, the score is used to indicate the internal states of the characters, such as the romantic feelings of the "Waikiki" and "He Needs Me" sequences.[85] Likewise, the pounding drums of the Hawaiian parade suggest Barry's anxiety before meeting Lena. As with Anderson's inclination to externalize the ego of a character, these uses of music in the film function to indicate to us a 'correct' emotional reading of the characters.

But this method of using music in *Punch-Drunk Love* is the less interesting, more straightforward method of emotional manipulation. The more important use of music is its function as keeper of the film's rhythm. Many times in *Punch-Drunk Love*, Anderson allows the harmonium to serve as our measuring stick of the harmony of Barry's life. For instance, when the phone sex operator makes repeated threatening phone calls, the bellows of the harmonium is ripped and Barry repairs the wound with tape. Nevertheless, Anderson does not allow the harmonium to function solely on a symbolic level. The film shows many sequences in which Barry plays along in tune with Jon Brion's dissonant soundtrack. This idea extends to other moments in *Punch-Drunk Love*, as inanimate objects often make sounds that harmonize with the film's score. For instance, when Barry and Lena are forced to leave the restaurant, a semi truck starts up and drives by them and its sounds are in tune with the romantic soundtrack. Anderson is making a point about a Zen-like relationship with the world by using this technique – that being in harmony with an individual translates into being in harmony with the world. He describes the theme of the film in musical terms: "It's about love, loneliness, becoming happy with yourself and comfortable with ourselves and trying to lose some insecurities and growing up...it's about getting in tune."[86] Moreover, there are several references to cosmic forces at work in the film (the truck that passes them is an Atlas Van Lines semi featuring a picture of a globe, Georgia watches footage of an astronaut landing while she talks with customers). Anderson even includes a nod to Frank Capra's *It's A Wonderful Life* in Jeremy Blake's color sequences that turn into twinkling stars, as if to say that Barry and Lena are guided by a sort of cosmic force. This is Anderson's larger point with *Punch-Drunk Love*, and one that has resonated in each of his films – that individual relationships are the most meaningful and that they are capable of re-harmonizing the universe.

CONCLUSION

Paul Thomas Anderson's films communicate a split that has occurred in the modern American. His films depict a world in which communication has been fractured into the meaningful and the artificial. This split in the human personality has created a void between a self that is based on trust and a self that is based on skepticism. The worlds of *Hard Eight*, *Boogie Nights*, *Magnolia* and *Punch-Drunk Love* are composite portraits of the human experience and monuments to the modern disposition, whereby individuals have been depersonalized by a system that seeks to suppress uniqueness and force conformity.

Many critics are quick to find a place for P.T. Anderson in a crowded independent film scene of the 1990s. One journalist sees Anderson as the antithesis of Tarantino: "There always seem to be such starkly oppositional figures in American culture as Tarantino and Anderson: dark, Gothic, austerely elitist Poe vs. all-embracing democratic Whitman."[87] This comparison may be unfair and reductive, as Anderson certainly has an inclination towards showmanship. If half of his films convey the humanism of Whitman, the other half of P.T. Anderson comes close to P.T. Barnum. However, the grander point is that Anderson is not interested *only* in style, but wants to ask us questions about why we do what we do. In each of his films, people are deeply troubled and are seeking a way out of the patterns they have created for themselves. Ultimately, Anderson rewards us with giving them an escape route, without expressing the same degree of cynicism about the world that Robert Altman or Jean-Luc Godard do. He does not allow the viewer to leave with a fatalistic message of despair, but rather, wants to affirm that human problems are not insurmountable. His films communicate a cosmological and spiritual connection that we all have to one another. This sense of connectivity, whether familial as in *Hard Eight*, *Boogie Nights*, and *Magnolia*, or romantic as in *Punch-Drunk Love*, ask that we recognize the importance of these connections in our own lives. They are ultimately hopeful films that present a celebratory attitude towards both the good and bad parts of the human experience.

WORKS CITED

Anderson, Paul Thomas. *Boogie Nights* Director's Commentary Soundtrack. New Line Home Video, 2000.

———. *Hard Eight* Director's Commentary Soundtrack. Columbia TriStar Home Video, 1999.

———. *Avant Premiere*. March 2000. Available from http://www.ptanderson.com/articlesandinterviews/avantpremiere.htm. Accessed 17 April 2004.

———. "The Charlie Rose Show." PBS Broadcasting. Original airdate: 30 October 1997.

———. "The Charlie Rose Show." PBS Broadcasting. Original airdate: 10 October 2002.

———. "People Online/AOL Chat with Anderson and Cheadle." 17 November 1997. Available from http://www.ptanderson.com/articlesandinterviews/peopleaolchat.htm. Accessed 17 April 2004.

———. Press Conference, Lisbon, Portugal, 5 February 2003. Transcription by Ruth Goncalves. Available from http://www.ptanderson.com/articlesandinterviews/pdl/portugal.htm. Accessed 17 April 2004.

Benedetti, Sandra. "Cinelive: March 2000," *Cinelive Magazine*. March 2000.

Braudy, Leo. *The World in a Frame: What We See in Films*. Chicago: University of Chicago Press, 2002.

Carney, Ray. Interviews with author. September 2003 – April 2004. Boston University College of Communication. Boston, Massachusetts.

Cox, Don. "It's Time for Reno to Star in New Movie," *Reno Gazette Journal*. 16 February 1995.

Donadoni, Serena. "Coincidental Breakdown," *Detroit Metro Times*, 5 January 2000.

Ebert, Roger. *Roger Ebert's Movie Yearbook, 1999*. Kansas City: Andrews McMeel Publishing, 1999.

Fuchs, Cynthia. *Addicted to Noise (AUSTRALIA)*, date unknown. Available from http://www.ptanderson.com/articlesandinterviews/addictedtonoise.htm. Accessed 17 April 2004.

Gilbey, Ryan. "Interview: Paul Thomas Anderson," *The Times (UK)*. 2 February 2003.

Grainger, Matt. "Cinemattractions Q & A with Paul Thomas Anderson." February 1998. Available from http://www.ptanderson.com/articlesandinterviews/cinemattractions.htm. Accessed 17 April 2004.

Hartl, John. "Writer Created from Sundance Project," *Seattle Times*. 3 March 1997.

Howell, Peter. "Punch in the Dark," *The Star*. 11 October 2002.

Kam, Nadine. "Practical Insanity," *Honolulu Star-Bulletin*. 7 November 2002.

Kehr, Dave. "A Poet of Love and Chaos in the Valley," *The New York Times*. 6 October 2002.

Kennedy, Mark. "Whiz Filmmaker Plows Familiar Ground," *The Associated Press*. 12 January 2000. Available from http://www.ptanderson.com/articlesandinterviews/ap.htm. Accessed 17 April 2004.

Lewis, Simon. "Chicks...Dicks and Porno Flicks," *Uncut Magazine*. February 1998.

Patterson, John. "Magnolia Nights," *The Age (Australia)*. 12 March 2000.

Rabinovitz, Mark. "Indiewire.com Interview at the New York Film Festival." 31 October 1997. Available from http://www.ptanderson.com/articlesandinterviews/indiewire.htm. Accessed 17 April 2004.

Reilly, John C. Interview by author. 15 November 2002. Boston University College of Fine Arts. Boston, Massachusetts.

Rensen, David. "20 Questions," *Playboy Magazine*. February 1998.

Shepard, Sadia. "'From Here To Houdini's House': The Emerging Filmmaker Conversations with Sundance Lab Fellows Paul Thomas Anderson," Sundance Online. Available from http://www.ptanderson.com/articlesandinterviews/sundanceinterview.htm. Accessed 17 April 2004.

Simon, Jeff. "Naked Talent," *Buffalo News.* 26 October 1997.

Smith, Gavin. "Sight and Sound Q & A," *Sight and Sound Magazine.* January 1998.

Stephens, Chuck. "Interview with Paul Thomas Anderson," in P.T. Anderson, *Magnolia: The Shooting Script.* New York: Newmarket Press, 2000.

Strauss, Bob. "Wising Up," *Boston Globe.* 2 January 2000.

Suchsland, Ruediger. "I'm a Damn Confused Person," *Artechock Film Magazine.* February 2000.

Thompson, Ben. "Blame It on the Boogie Man," *Telegraph Magazine.* 3 January 1998.

Thompson, Bob. "Get Down and Boogie," *Toronto Sun.* October 1997.

Thompson, Gary. "X Marks the Spot," Philadelphia Daily News. 17 October 1997.

ENDNOTES

[1] Paul Thomas Anderson named his production company 'Ghoulardi Films' as a tribute to his late father's legacy.

[2] *Hard Eight* is the title that Rysher Entertainment, the film's distributor, gave to Anderson's film. The original script title, which Anderson prefers, was *Sydney*. But to avoid confusion, I use the title *Hard Eight* when referring to the film.

[3] Sadia Shepard, "'From Here To Houdini's House': The Emerging Filmmaker Conversations with Sundance Lab Fellows Paul Thomas Anderson," Sundance Online. Available from http://www.ptanderson.com/articlesandinterviews/sundanceinterview.htm.

[4] ibid.

[5] ibid.

[6] ibid.

[7] P.T. Anderson, DVD Commentary, *Hard Eight*. Columbia TriStar Home Video, 1999.

[8] As Reilly later told me, Anderson had noticed him years before in his earliest roles, including his acting debut in *Casualties of War* (1989) and could recite all of his lines from the actor's previous work at a time when Reilly's career was sputtering. This information comes from a discussion with John C. Reilly at Boston University's College of Fine Arts, 15 November 2002.

[9] ibid.

[10] John Hartl, "Writer Created from Sundance Project," in *Seattle Times*, 3 March 1997.

[11] Shepard, Sundance Online.

[12] ibid.

[13] DVD Commentary, *Hard Eight*.

[14] ibid.

[15] Don Cox, "It's Time for Reno to Star in New Movie," in *Reno Gazette Journal*, 16 February 1995.

[16] Hartl, "Writer Created from Sundance Project."

[17] DVD Commentary, *Hard Eight*.

[18] Shepard, Sundance Online.

[19] Chuck Stephens, "Interview with Paul Thomas Anderson," in P.T. Anderson, *Magnolia: The Shooting Script*, (New York: Newmarket Press, 2000), 203.

[20] Cox, "It's Time for Reno to Star in New Movie."

[21] As Anderson recalls the story that inspired the scene: "I was outside of Reno and my car broke down and a tow truck driver picked me up and told me that story. That was 1991."

[22] Anderson's original script included a scene in which the hostage from the hotel catches up with Sydney and kills him in the parking lot of the restaurant.

[23] Matt Grainger, "Cinemattractions Q & A with Paul Thomas Anderson," available online at http://www.ptanderson.com/articlesandinterviews/cinemattractions.htm, February 1998.

[24] Discussion with John C. Reilly, Boston University College of Fine Arts, 15 November 2002.

[25] "The Charlie Rose Show," Original Airdate: 30 October 1997.

[26] David Rensen, "20 Questions," in *Playboy Magazine*, February 1998.

[27] People Online/AOL Chat with Anderson and Cheadle, 17 November 1997.

[28] Discussion with John C. Reilly, Boston University College of Fine Arts, 15 November 2002.

[29] Ben Thompson, "Blame It on the Boogie Man," in *Telegraph Magazine*, 3 January 1998.

[30] Simon Lewis, "Chicks…Dicks and Porno Flicks," in *Uncut Magazine*, February 1998.

[31] Roger Ebert, *Roger Ebert's Movie Yearbook, 1999*, (Kansas City: Andrews McMeel Publishing, 1999).

[32] "The Charlie Rose Show," Original Airdate: 30 October 1997.

[33] Anderson cites his biggest influences as 1970s independent film icons Robert Altman and Martin Scorsese. But Anderson does not take stylistically from these directors as much as one might imagine. The influence is most evident in the confidence to be what Anderson calls "punk rock" in his filmmaking. He realized that one could do anything and that it did not necessarily need to make sense.

[34] Gavin Smith, "Sight and Sound Q & A," in *Sight and Sound Magazine*, January 1998.

[35] ibid.

[36] Gary Thompson, "X Marks the Spot," in *Philadelphia Daily News*, 17 October 1997.

[37] Cynthia Fuchs, *Addicted to Noise (AUSTRALIA)*, date unknown. Available from http://www.ptanderson.com/articlesandinterviews/addictedtonoise.htm.

[38] This appears in an intertitle in the final sequence of the film, which reads, "One last thing—long way down."

[39] Mark Rabinovitz, "Indiewire.com Interview," 31 October 1997. Available from http://www.ptanderson.com/articlesandinterviews/indiewire.htm.

[40] Smith, "Sight and Sound Q & A."

[41] ibid.

[42] This idea comes from a discussion of *Boogie Nights* held on 13 April 2004 at Boston University's College of Communication with Professor Ray Carney.

[43] P.T. Anderson, *Boogie Nights DVD Commentary Track*. New Line Home Video, 2000.

[44] Films like Quentin Tarantino's *Reservoir Dogs* and *Pulp Fiction* and Kevin Smith's *Clerks* are films more concerned with genre convention and representative characterizations. This was partly due to the legacy of 1960s and 1970s studio independent films (*Easy Rider, Midnight Cowboy, Bonnie and Clyde*), coming from a tradition that sought to capture the sentiment of a moment in American history rather than deal with human emotions. *Boogie Nights* is a film out of this same tradition, but attempts to mix personal drama with the definition of a cultural moment.

[45] John Patterson, "Magnolia Nights," in *The Age*, 12 March 2000.

[46] ibid.

[47] ibid.

[48] Serena Donadoni, "Coincidental Breakdown," in *Metro Times*, 5 January 2000.

[49] Just before he burglarizes his work, Donnie Smith looks in the mirror and says, "You know, you know, you know, go, go, go." Likewise, during Frank's interview with Gwenovier, Mackey says, "Go, go, go...I am firing pearls at you here."

[50] Mark Kennedy, "Whiz Filmmaker Plows Familiar Ground," in *The Associated Press*, 12 January 2000.

[51] Bob Strauss, "Wising Up," in *Boston Globe*, 2 January 2000.

[52] Ruediger Suchsland, "I'm a Damn Confused Person," in *Artechock Film Magazine*, February 2000.

[53] Donadoni, "Coincidental Breakdown."

[54] For instance, Altman's *Short Cuts*, a film often cited in correlation to *Magnolia*, ends with a cataclysmic earthquake that covers the murder of a young woman. In Godard's *Weekend*, a trip into the country is littered with the post-apocalyptic remains of a self-destructed society.

[55] Sandra Benedetti, "Cinelive: March 2000," in *Cinelive Magazine*, March 2000. Consequently, it is interesting that Anderson admires and takes from the films of Robert Altman, whose films were known in the 1970s for an unprecedented degree of cynicism.

[56] There are a few moments in which Anderson uses humor to lighten scene. When Earl is dying, Anderson inserts "Also sprach Zarathustra," recalling the final sequence of *2001: A Space Odyssey*. Additionally, the game show announcer states that "What Do Kids Know?" is endorsed by the PTA – his initials. We are meant to catch these references, as Anderson wants to occasionally remind us that we are watching a film. This is a tactic that he uses to avoid sinking into an over-sentimentalized scene.

[57] This idea comes from a discussion with critic Ray Carney at Boston University's College of Communication, November 2003.

[58] Coincidentally, Anderson worked briefly as a production assistant in the early 1990s on a quiz show in Los Angeles, which pitted gifted children against adult challengers.

[59] Strauss, "Wising Up."

[60] *Magnolia* owes a lot structurally to Griffith's film. Each film crosscuts between several different narratives and is connected by theme rather than plot. As with the game show in *Magnolia*, *Intolerance* repeatedly goes back to an anchor sequence of Lillian Gish rocking the cradle of time.

Like *Magnolia*, it was considered by many to be a train wreck of a film which confused contemporary audiences and failed at the box office.

[61] Leo Braudy, *The World in a Frame: What We See in Films*, (Chicago: University of Chicago Press, 2002), 46.

[62] George Thomas, "Success Blossoms for *Magnolia* Director," in *Akron-Beacon Journal*, 7 January 2000.

[63] Donadoni, "Coincidental Breakdown."

[64] ibid.

[65] Braudy, *The World in a Frame: What We See in Films*, 47.

[66] *Avant Premiere*, March 2000. Available from http://www.ptanderson.com/articlesandinterviews/avantpremiere.htm.

[67] This technique has a long tradition in the American Cinema of the 1960s and 1970s, beginning with "Mrs. Robinson" in *The Graduate*. The films of Robert Altman also frequently utilize music on the soundtrack to comment on the action of the characters, as in *Nashville*.

[68] Suchsland, "I'm a Damn Confused Person."

[69] Press Conference, Lisbon, Portugal, 5 February 2003. Transcription by Ruth Goncalves. Available from http://www.ptanderson.com/articlesandinterviews/pdl/portugal.htm.

[70] Stanley Kubrick, while filming *Eyes Wide Shut*, discussed the benefits of a small crew with Anderson. Not only did working with fewer people help the actors, but helped Anderson relax on the set without the commotion of a standard Hollywood shoot.

[71] Peter Howell, "Punch in the Dark," in *The Star*, 11 October 2002.

[72] The comfortability between the seven sisters is evident in the kitchen dinner scene. Anderson recalls many times when he would yell "Cut!" and the actresses would simply keep talking and preparing the food.

[73] Press Conference, Lisbon, Portugal, February 5, 2003.

[74] This desire to avoid over-sentimentalizing is a common trait shared by many of Anderson's contemporary American independent directors, a characteristic that many critics attribute to the perceived cynicism and anti-sentimentality of the Gen-X slacker generation.

[75] Anderson is attempting to portray the type of love seen in films like John Cassavetes' *Minnie and Moskowitz*, where love is measured by intensity rather by clearly defined positive or negative actions. Often in *Punch-Drunk Love* and *Minnie and Moskowitz*, a character will express love in a way that might seem excessive or even dangerous.

[76] Dave Kehr, "A Poet of Love and Chaos in the Valley," in *The New York Times*, 6 October 2002.

[77] Ryan Gilbey, "Interview: Paul Thomas Anderson," in *The Times (UK)*, 2 February 2003.

[78] Kehr, "A Poet of Love and Chaos in the Valley."

[79] In a deleted sequence, the camera lingers on the Hawaiian dancers for an extended scene.

[80] For example, Marion Crane's nervousness manifests itself as rain in *Psycho*. In *Rear Window*, Mr. Jeffries' neighbors are all variations of Lisa Fremont, his girlfriend. In these films, Hitchcock gives us the impression that our ego is strong enough to control our immediate environment. This is not the case in the world of Jean Renior, in whose films the characters' egos and desires conflict and interact. *This idea comes from discussions with critic Ray Carney at Boston University's College of Communication in April 2004.*

[81] In *Magnolia*, the sadness of a character can cause the weather to change. In *Boogie Nights*, Eddie's bedroom décor expresses the internal psychology of his character.

[82] Ray Carney, Boston University's College of Communication, April 2004.

[83] Nadine Kam, "Practical Insanity," in *Honolulu Star-Bulletin*, 7 November 2002.

[84] ibid.

[85] The "He Needs Me" song comes directly from Shelley Duvall's rendition in Robert Altman's 1980 film *Popeye*.

[86] "The Charlie Rose Show," Original airdate: 10 October 2002.

[87] Jeff Simon, "Naked Talent," in *Buffalo News*, 26 October 1997.